Integrating Careers Into Your Classroom: Past, Present, and Future

By Dr. Bonnie-Marie Doughty-Jenkins

Green Heart Living Press

Integrating Careers Into Your Classroom: Past, Present, and Future

Copyright © 2021 Dr. Bonnie-Marie Doughty-Jenkins

All rights reserved. No part of this book may be used or reproduced by any means, graphic, electronic, or mechanical, including photocopying, recording, taping or by any information storage retrieval system without the written permission of the publisher, except in the case of brief quotations embodied in critical articles and reviews.

ISBN Paperback: 978-1-954493-12-4

Dedication

This book is dedicated to the following:

~ My parents for their constant support of all my endeavors

~ All "like-minded" people who agree with my vision

~ Friends, Family and Colleagues who have helped along the way

~ Mr. David Robins for making me want to become an educator and Dr. Daniel Mulcahy for assuring me that my research has merit

~ My husband, John, who I hope is looking down on me with pride…NEM

LB

Table of Contents

Foreword	7
Introduction	9
Chapter 1: Defining School-to-Career	13
Chapter 2: National History and Trends	17
Chapter 3: Perspectives Regarding School-to-Career	25
Chapter 4: Interview Results	35
Chapter 5: Analysis and Critique	37
Chapter 6: The Future	47
Appendix A	49
Appendix B	55
References	63

Foreword

Successful careers are defined differently for everyone.

Many of us demanded that our children follow in the footsteps of their family members. Many of us demanded that our children become the person that we wanted to be, and others demanded a college education of their children. All of these demands have certainly created strain on families across America over the last 50 plus years.

America is the land of opportunities, but the American school system is not currently aligned to translate what those opportunities are, past, present, and future.

You will find that this book contains many facts, attempted solutions, and tools for educators to engage students, creating a more positive teaching experience. If a teacher can open a world of opportunity through career exploration, it will change those students forever.

In over 35 years of partnering with schools to recruit high school students for opportunities in the manufacturing industry, I found that my vision was not shared by many manufacturers early in my career because students did not bring experience to the table. We know today that manufacturing is now seeing that their delay in partnering with schools to communicate their needs has created a large void in the labor pool. We are finding that the need for experience is not as strong in 2021. Employers will now train because they need to train to satisfy customer demand. Industry moves fast and school systems move slowly.

College is not for everyone, but education in some format is for everyone. How one learns is unique to the individual and identifying it at a young age makes the selection of higher learning so much easier. My experience in being a Human Resources professional and Student to Career Strategist/Coach has opened my eyes to so much that is misaligned in the school to career arena and how few people within school and industry desired to pay attention to the opportunity until it became a real time problem.

As Dr. Bonnie-Marie Doughty-Jenkins mentions in this book, it is predicted that there will be over six million skilled trade vacancies by 2028.

How I wish that this book would have been around as I toured so many schools in Connecticut, helping to educate teachers and students on the opportunities that live within the manufacturing industry. I am grateful that Dr. Bonnie-Marie Doughty-Jenkins has taken the time to document the hits and misses showing the divide of support for school-to-career over the years. This book will help bring educators to an understanding of how we arrived at today, a true skilled labor crisis. I have seen it, I've felt it, and I've helped to work around it by training teenagers while other businesses were waiting for the experienced candidate to walk through the door.

This book provides 30 years of valuable shared insight and information. Dr. Bonnie-Marie Doughty-Jenkins experienced the void from an educator's perspective, and I experienced the void from an industry level. This book reveals past, present, and future fixes to the crisis that has been brewing for over 25 years. Let's connect students with their learning style at a young age and create offerings that stimulate their passions, making education an experience that future employers can respect and trust as not all students will be making traditional college part of their life plans.

      Thanks, Dr. Bonnie-Marie Doughty-Jenkins. It is truly an honor to be asked to write this foreword.

Lori Theriault
CEO & Founder
WORK IT!
Workitcareers.com

Introduction

Having been in education for over 30 years, I have noticed something: testing is king and most districts are focused on students going onto college. A passion of mine for most of my career has been that not everyone needs to go to college. Don't mistake what I am saying, people need to be EDUCATED. That education is just not always through the college route. Along the way, I have found some like-minded people to help me with my mission and they have additionally helped me champion my cause. I believe in this vision so much that it was the topic of my doctoral dissertation.

School-to-Career is not a topic usually taught in teacher education courses yet it has been around since the time of Plato. Although it has morphed over time, it is still as relevant today as it always has been. This book is meant to follow that historical perspective up to where it is today and guide people as to its validity in the future.

Background

Worthington & Juntunen (1997) have suggested that, because there has been much inadequate preparation of students for careers and the workforce prior to leaving high school, many high school graduates struggle in the world of work. They argue that students who graduate without any type of career education program can flounder in "dead end" jobs with no hope for advancement and little opportunity for career development or improvement. Research shows that school-to-career initiatives improve attendance and participation in school, which, in turn, increase performance (Coomer 1999; Harmon, 1999; United States Department of Labor Employment and Training Administration, 1994; Worthington & Juntunen, 1997). These initiatives give a sense of purpose to students to attend school and give them a connection to the world outside of school. Students can see the direct benefits of their schooling.

Nationwide school-to-career initiatives since the 1980s are a step in the direction of creating programs to prepare youth for their future careers. At the federal level, there have been several legislative and other governmental initiatives, such as the Perkins Act (1990), School-to-Work Opportunities Act (STWOA) (1994), the Secretary's Commission on Achieving Necessary Skills (SCANS) (2000), and a portion of Goals 2000: Educate America Act (1994). There has also been research on school-to-career initiatives at the national level (Brand, Partee, Kaufmann, & Willis, 2000; Castellano, Stringfield, & Stone, 2003; Evans & Burck, 1992; Gitterman, Levi, & Wayne, 1995; Glover & Marshall, 1993; Johnson, 2000; Kazis, 1999; Lynch, 2000; Tiederman, 1975; U. S. Department of Labor Employment and Training Administration, 1994).

On the face of it, the school-to-career initiatives taken may appear to be a welcome development of both policy and practice. There has not been much research carried out on the matter, however. One piece of research that does exist is a field study conducted in the Plymouth School District during the 2002-2003 school year (Doughty-Jenkins, 2003). In addition, there are the three reports published by Abt Associates for the Connecticut State Department of Education, Bureau of Career and Adult Education (October 2001, June 2003, & July 2003).

The problem addressed and the justification for this research emerged from the absence of research into them. We have no clear overall understanding of what has been happening in the area of school-to-career transitions. In the interest of evaluating state educational policy and improving school practice, it is highly desirable that we should have this understanding. The chief significance of this book lies in providing such understanding. The focus is on the investigation and analysis of the school-to-career initiative since 1990 with a view to describing its course of development, identifying its distinguishing features, analyzing its strengths and weaknesses, and reflecting on the policy issues that arise. It is anticipated that this (a) will contribute to the advancement of knowledge in the field, (b) will make available to educators and public policy makers in Connecticut a resource that may guide further investigations in the field, (c) will discover new knowledge and (d) will provide a point of reference for those wishing to consider and implement change at the state and local levels.

Purpose and Scope

The purpose of this book is to describe and analyze the policies and activities associated with the beginnings and subsequent development of the school-to-career movement since 1990. The scope was determined by the variety of agencies involved (including schools, school boards, the Connecticut State Department of Education, and the CBIA), the policies by which these agencies were guided, relevant legislation, personal interviews, and the broader knowledge base identified in a review of literature dealing with the topic on national and international levels.

Nationally-conducted research is used to gain relevant perspectives on developments in School-to Career. The interpretation these perspectives put on such matters often differs greatly from that found in legislation at both the state and federal levels of the past two plus decades. Consequently, it can enable the researcher to draw attention to aspects of the relationship between school and career that may not be found in government policies dealing with the matter.

Based on a wide-ranging review of relevant national research literature, the book identifies relevant research studies and describes legislative initiatives in the United States. It identifies, for comparison and analysis, themes of significance for the topic of school-to-career that emerge in the literature. Examples of such themes include the evolutionary nature of the notion of preparation for work or school-to-work; the interplay between this and career or school counseling; the emergence of a systems approach, guiding principles, and assumptions in dealing with school-to-career; the place of teamwork between schools and places of work; the experience of "school-to-career" in the college setting; and indicators from research for policy making and program development.

The record of debate, policy, action, and inaction at both the district and state levels are considered in this context. Arising from this, issues of significance for educational policy in

Connecticut are identified. Attention is given, where appropriate, to issues of gender, ability levels and socio-economic status.

Approach/Methods and Procedures

The approach employed in this book may be broadly described as qualitative. It does not employ the full range of the many methodologies or approaches commonly associated with qualitative research, such as action research, ethnography, and grounded theory. Rather, it employs a combination of descriptive and analytical methodologies. Because there is an emphasis on the study of documents, it makes greatest use of forms of inquiry associated with literary criticism, historical research, and some conceptual analysis. In addition, semi-structured interviews from various entities within school-to-career programs are used and interpreted to gain various perspectives with regard to school-to-career programs.

Nature of the Research Base and Sources

Original sources, based on interviews, and what may be termed "primary sources" and "secondary sources" are used. Primary sources include legislation at the state and federal levels; official documents from government agencies such as the United States Department of Labor. Secondary sources include scholarly journals and relevant research. Finally, the main types of original sources used are semi-structured interviews conducted for the purpose of this research in addition to an original field study conducted.

Chapter 1: Defining School-to-Career

Career development is defined as an integral aspect of human development as a whole. According to the U.S. Department of Labor Employment and Training Administration, the main objective of school-to-work programs is "raising students' career and educational aspirations or at least exposing students to new options and opportunities." (1994, p. 32) Gysbers and Moore believe that "this expanded view of the career concept is more appropriate than the traditional view of career as an occupational choice. It is more appropriate because it breaks the time barrier that previously restricted the vision of career to only a cross-sectional view of an individual's life." (1975, p. 647) This helps one to realize that there is a difference between an occupation (meaning what one does) and a career (meaning a course pursued over time). In 2000, the United States Department of Labor Employment and Training Administration defined school-to-work as representing "a potentially important improvement in the nation's efforts to fully prepare its young people for successful and productive careers." (p. ES-1) America as a whole has changed from a rural society to a complex industrial one. This has been the impetus for the changing of the definition of the whole concept of career.

Worthington & Juntunen (1997) believe that because there has been such inadequate preparation of students prior to leaving high school, many graduates struggle in the world of work. They argue that students who graduate without any type of career education program will flounder in "dead-end" jobs with no hope for advancement and little opportunity for a career. One would assume that creating a career education opportunity would be the work of a counselor. This is not always the case. "Despite the fact that counseling psychology, as a profession, has been intimately involved with the field of career development since its inception, attempts to link counseling psychology and the school-to-work movement are almost non-existent." (Worthington & Juntunen, 1997, p.323) This is contrary to the belief that these professionals could have so many varied and unique contributions to the world of the school-to-work movement. According to Worthington and Juntunen (1997), the school-to-work movement, if continuing as it started, could easily affect the lives of at least 75% of youth. It would appear that the counselors need to get more educated as to where these trends are heading.

It is theorized by Worthington and Juntunen (1997), that career education can be placed on a continuum of concepts. These concepts are job, work, self, and life, with job being the least desirable on the continuum. "Job" refers to occupational training. This is essentially training a person to do a specific job. This is the least desirable because there is no personal satisfaction in it and it is strictly a repetitive process with no meaning. "Work" refers to occupational preparation. This is more satisfying and intellectually stimulating than a job. It is part of the educational process. Although it does require some skill training, it goes beyond that with the inclusion of post-secondary education. "Self" insinuates that work can be either a paid or volunteer opportunity. It focuses more on the way that the people not only explore their options but the way that they interact within the context of their chosen field. A career should help you to create a purposeful life pattern. The final concept is that of life. "Life" refers to a way of viewing career education as a part of the total education. It is believed that by restructuring curriculum and programs that people can advocate for and accomplish reforms to educate for life as a whole.

The Minnesota Career Development Curriculum identifies six basic principles to self-based career programs:

> *First, career development is a lifelong process of self-development, work being viewed as a vehicle for self-clarification. Second, career development includes the opportunity to examine life roles, occupations, and lifestyles. Third, the process of life-span career development and decision making is emphasized more than the choice itself. Fourth, management of one's career, the power to direct one's future, the ability to maximize control over one's life is a major tenet. Fifth, the concept of multipotentiality – that each person has the potential for success and satisfaction in a number of occupations – frees individuals from the fear of making wrong choices and increases their available options. Sixth, commitment with tentativeness is a concept that is integral to a model based on changing individuals and society and that recognizes the importance of chance factors in career decisions. (Hansen & Tennyson, 1975, p.641)*

A comprehensive career education program may need to incorporate several principles throughout the entire K-12 curriculum. These include problem solving, understanding of self and others, understanding the world as a whole, obtaining skills and experiences, and achieving self-identity. "Ways need to be found to incorporate the salient principles of career development into an integrated program that focuses on the self-development of individuals and the tasks facing them as they move through various stages of career over the life span." (Hansen & Tennyson, 1975, p.638)

What should School-to-Career be? According to the State of Connecticut, Department of Education (2002):

> *A School-to-Career System is a comprehensive system of education that allows all students the opportunity to connect the learning in the classroom to the needs and demands of higher education and the workplace. Every School-to-Career system must contain three core elements known as school-based learning, work-based learning, and connecting activities as well as be organized around industry-development career clusters (p.1)*

It is believed that students in their sophomore year of high school should have been adequately exposed to these career clusters. They should be able to make an educated decision as to where their career goals lie. These Career Clusters vary from state to state and can range anywhere from 8 to 18 clusters. The 16 Career Clusters that are endorsed by the United States Department of Education are: Agriculture, Food & Natural Resources; Architecture & Construction; Arts, Audio/Video Technology & Communications; Business, Management & Administration; Education & Training; Finance; Government & Public Administration; Health Science; Hospitality & Tourism; Human Services; Information Technology; Law, Public Safety, Corrections & Security; Manufacturing; Marketing, Sales & Service; Science, Technology, Engineering & Mathematics and Transportation, Distribution & Logistics.

It is the hope that the exposure to the career clusters will be a useful tool for potential employers to use because they will know that this particular person has been appropriately exposed to employability and practical skills for the position that is being offered.

In addition, the United States Department of Labor Employment and Training Administration (2000) suggests four important aspects of any school-to-work program as a basis for its very definition. These four areas are (1) recruitment and counseling, (2) school-based learning, (3) work-based learning, and (4) connecting activities. These areas should be encompassed as a part of the program as a way to track progress and develop a system of continuous improvement.

Chapter 2: National History and Trends

What is School-to-Career? According to Kazis (1999) "School-to-Career is a broad umbrella [term] covering many different forms of collaboration between schools and workplaces." (p.16)

The history and research on this topic has been extensive. Throughout history, people have believed that there should be education for future careers, and more recently, that this is the government's responsibility. As a matter of fact, education for career has been of concern dating back to the time of Plato who believed that people should be educated in order to prepare themselves for their intended futures. Early in United States' history, Thomas Jefferson argued for education that would prepare citizens for their potential careers as citizens and politicians.

In 1909, Frank Parsons (1854-1909) wrote a book titled *Choosing a Vocation*. This book is considered one of the first to truly emphasize the importance of making transitions from school to work. In this Parsons attempted to change the perceptions of the way people viewed school-to-work. He popularized the concept of vocational development rather than a "mindless" training of individuals for rote processes. He organized and was director of the Vocation Bureau of Boston. As director of this bureau, he is credited with being the first to coin the phrase "vocational guidance". He developed the concept of the vocational guidance triangle, and believed that vocational guidance should involve three parts: the individual, the employment, and the correlation of the two. From the work of Parsons grew the Department of Vocational Guidance which was created in 1915. The focus of this department was to successfully integrate and strengthen the relationship of the vocational guidance triangle. At that time, there were three basic kinds of preparation that a person could get. They could attend Latin schools, which led to college, high schools which lead to either a factory or college, and trade school, which lead into the world of industry. Boston was looked upon as a district that was at the forefront of vocational education and vocational guidance. This cemented Parsons' place as the "Godfather of School-to Career Education."

John Dewey, the well-known 20th century educator, believed that education should have a basis in the "real world". He "described reasons to be concerned with educational improvement, two of which continue to stand out at the dawn of the 21st century: furthering democratic ideals through a broadly educated citizenry, and obtaining a viable economic future for all citizens." (Catellano, Stringfield, & Stone, 2003, p.239) According to Dewey, career education should not focus on a particular career. For him, "such occupation – based projects 'should never educate *for* vocations, but should educate *through* vocations." (Tozer, Violas, and Senese, 2002, p. 108-109)

Between 1915 and 1930, Charles W. Eliot began writing about education. Eliot believed that it was important for people to gain skills that would help them in their future employment and that vocational education would help them attain this goal. (Tozer, Violas, and Senese, 2002) Eliot believed vocational education should not only provide actual skills for a particular trade but also other skills that would help individuals in the world of work such as basic social graces.

Eliot's writing influenced Congress and aided in the passage of the Smith-Hughes Act of 1917, the first major federal legislation that dealt with the School-to-Work movement. This legislation was the first effort by the federal government to finance career education. In addition, Eliot aided in having this groundbreaking act passed. He believed that it was important for people to gain skills that would help them in their future employment and that vocational education would help them attain this goal. (Tozer, Violas, and Senese, 2002, p. 110-111) This act was essentially designed to aid pre-collegiate education and was the first federal legislation of its type. (Wirth, 2004) In addition, the Smith-Hughes Act established a Federal Board for Vocational Education that was separate from the United States Office of Education and was only responsible to Congress. (Wirth, 2004, ¶2) The act annually appropriated funds to the States to cooperate with them and to assist in the "paying of salaries of teachers, supervisors, and directors of agricultural subjects, and teachers of trade, home economics and industrial subjects, and in the preparation of teachers of agriculture, trade, industrial and home economics subjects." (Smith-Hughes Act, 1917, §1¶2) The states had to create a State board with all members having the power to cooperate and interact with the Federal Board for Vocational Education in administrating the act. Any state was allowed to take advantage of this new legislation. However, it was written into the act that any state that wanted to take advantage of the availability of these funds had to give teachers in those areas the minimum amount of training in order to receive these funds. It is interesting to note that these funds were also to include "vocational coursework for young women" (Bernard-Powers, 2004, ¶1) such as typing, stenography, bookkeeping, and home economics.

According to Section Six of the Smith-Hughes Act, the Federal Board for Vocational Education that was to be formed would consist of:

> *the Secretary of Agriculture, the Secretary of Commerce, the Secretary of Labor, the United States Commissioner of Education and three citizens of the United States to be appointed by the President, by and with the advice and consent of the Senate. One of said three citizens shall be a representative of the manufacturing and commercial interests, one a representative of the agricultural interests, and one a representative of labor. (Smith-Hughes Act, 1917, §6¶1)*

This Board also conducted studies and investigations as well as created reports that were a concern of many entities within the Federal Government, including agriculture, commerce, and education. Because agriculture was the prevailing occupational field during this era, it was included that at the minimum, in order to receive funding, the schools "shall provide for directed or supervised practice in agriculture, either on a farm provided for by the school or other farm, for at least six months per year." (Smith-Hughes Act, 1917, §10) In addition, it is also relevant to remember that portions of this act also applied to home economics and industrial education. The focus of these programs, in order to receive funding, had to be for students over 14 years of age who were not going to be going to a college and therefore needed this type of educational training to assist them with their future roles in society. According to Dr. Charles Prosser, the Smith-Hughes Act was to help a person "secure a job, train him so he can hold it after he gets it and assist him in advancing to a better job." (Wirth, 2004, p. 3) The training was purely job specific and was essentially non–transferable to any other occupations or fields. This act stayed in effect as it was written until it was eventually amended in 1963.

It is important to note that in the early 1900's, women still did not have the right to vote in the United States. Upon receiving this right in 1920 there was:

> *a broad-based campaign to increase funding for women's vocational education [resulting] in a substantial increase in federal monies expended on 'vocational home economics'. By 1930 home economics had a permanent and federally assisted place in public junior and senior high schools in the United States.* (Bernard-Powers, 2004, ¶4)

The earliest cooperative education models can be traced back to Dayton, Ohio in 1913. Programs gave high school students the opportunity for on the job training by putting them in placements that would be on a short term basis. According to the U.S. Department of Labor, Employment and Training Administration, one of the major shortcomings of this type of program is "that students often develop specialized skills needed by one employer but fail to learn more generalizable skills." (1994, p. 5) They also argue that these programs do not have an effect on the curriculum and do not help to bridge the gap of what is learned in school and the "real world."

James B. Conant, another pioneer in career education, believed that vocational education should be part of every high school's curriculum and not be limited to being a part of the curriculum of vocational schools. (Tozer, Violas, and Senese, 2002) According to Tozer, Violas, and Senese (2002), "Conant clearly argued that such a separation was inadvisable and that a comprehensive high school should offer different kinds of curricula under the same roof." (p.331)

Much of the more popular literature in the field of career education began to emerge during the 1950's. Prior to that time, much of what practitioners focused on related more to the occupational aspects of the School-to-Career system. As a matter of fact, up until the 1950's, the whole concept was referred to as "school-to-work." This often had a negative connotation, especially in the inner cities because it appeared as if the inner city students were directed toward a world of "work" rather than toward the possibility of college and a "career." It is also important to realize that in the mid-century, the economy of the United States was still based on manufacturing and natural resources, and people could go into the job market right out of high school with a position that could last a lifetime. Toward the end of this decade, work environments began to "require workers who (could) analyze data, communicate with precision, deal with ambiguity, learn rapidly, participate in what were considered management decisions in hierarchical management systems, and work well in teams." (Glover & Marshall, 1993, p.591-592) Also at this time, E. Ginzberg began a movement to try to better organize the field of career psychology. A major step in this reform was his writing of the book *The Psychology of Careers* in 1957. "It changed the study of vocational psychology from that of singular vocational events into that of the interactive and multitudinous vocational events that occur from birth to death." (Tiederman, 1975, p.706)

In the sixties, career education started to show itself as a prominent theme in counseling. Counselors often encouraged people who were not "college bound" to explore more of the hands-on careers in factories and manufacturing that were abundant during that era. At this time, in Philadelphia the concept of "youth academies" began to develop. These are also referred to as schools within schools. These academies were designed for 10th to 12th grade students. Within these academies, "students in each grade take most or all of their courses together, including core academic subjects and a practical lab in technology relevant to the occupational focus. Local employers help design the technical part of their curriculum and donate necessary equipment, provide volunteer mentors, and give students summer jobs between grades 11 and 12." (U.S. Department of Labor Employment and Training Administration, 1994, p.5) According to Gysbers and Moore (1975):

> *prior to the 1950's theorists and practitioners had focused most of their attention on the occupational aspects of the transition from school to work...During the 1950's, theorists began to emphasize a developmental view of occupational choice. It was during this period that the term vocational development became popular as a way of describing the broadened view of occupational choice and the many factors that influenced it. (p. 647)*

Included among these new views of vocation and career is Ginzberg's work with the field of Career Psychology, which was also a major factor at this point in the history of school-to-career initiatives. Axelrad, Herma, and Ginzberg wrote a book titled *Occupational Choice: An Approach to General Theory* in 1951. This book dealt with the developmental stages of people from childhood to young adulthood. According to the writings of Axelrad, Herma and Ginzberg, "in those stages the occupational choice is supposed to advance from the condition of fantasy into the condition of reality and preliminary trial." (Tiederman, 1975, p. 706) Also according to Tiederman (1975), D. E. Super's theory of vocational development and 10 propositions which were created in 1953 were a direct result of the Ginzberg book. (p. 706)

Another major national influence on career education is the work of James B. Conant, including his writing of *Education and Liberty* in 1953 and *The American High School Today* in 1958. According to Tozer, Violas, & Senese, 2002:

> *He believed that the public high school should enroll students preparing for vocations along with those preparing for college, but his rationale was largely social, not educational....It would forge closer relationships among future professional people, craftspersons, engineers, and labor leaders and help promote "not only equality of opportunity but equality of esteem in all forms of labor. (p. 234)*

According to Wirth (2004):

> *The critics of the 1960's identified two central failures of vocational education: (1) its lack of sensitivity to changes in the labor market, and (2) its lack of sensitivity to the needs of various segments of population. Critics charged that Smith-Hughes programs had been confined to a very narrow part of the spectrum of work activities and had failed to make imaginative adaptations to the demands of a fast changing economy. By concentrating on the job requirements of industry and by restricting its efforts to secondary school age students, Smith-Hughes also failed to give priority to the vocational needs of all groups in the community. The 1963 Act announced as its aim the development of vocational education for persons of all ages in all communities. This was to be accomplished with a unified concept of vocational education, rather than by sharply separated programs for vocational education. Special attention was to be paid to the needs*

of disadvantaged persons who had dropped out of school, lacked basic education skills, or needed re-training. (p.5)

During the 1970's, the field moved from "vocational" education to "career" education. This change was in name only, considering that the curriculum itself changed very little. This was also an era where many low-income, minority, and special education students were "encouraged" to go to vocational schools or "trade school" because it was believed that they would not "make it" in post-high school education. In 1971, the United States Commissioner of Education, Sidney P. Marland, Jr. announced at a convention of the National Association of Secondary School Principals (NASSP) that he believed that the purpose of education was to create a process that prepares the youth to be alive and active in their hearts as well as their hands. This was interpreted by many as Marland being a proponent of vocational education and career psychology. He continued to inform the members of the NASSP that they needed to understand the relationships of others and how those relationships can help build up skills needed for their futures. Prior to this time, standardized tests were the essential techniques for assessing students and for career planning. There weren't many programs that worked with the students on an individual basis.

It was during the 1980's where three basic goals of the career education movement came into play. These goals were identified as "(a) to change the educational system by inserting a "careers" emphasis throughout curriculum; (b) to make career education a joint effort with the community, rather than an effort of the educational system alone; and (c) to provide students with a set of general skills for adjusting to the changes in this occupational society." (Evans & Burck, 1992, p.63)

The next major piece of federal school-to-work legislation was the Carl D. Perkins Vocational and Education Act of 1990 (the Perkins Act). This act states that, "Each State board receiving funds under this act shall develop and implement a statewide system of core standards and measures of performance for secondary and postsecondary career education programs." (Perkins Act, 1990, §115a) This act required standards and measurements as well as program evaluations and plans for program improvement including a yearly self-evaluation of the plan. This was the beginning of moving from a system of simply teaching specific requirements for a narrowly defined job slot to a system of teaching skills that are transferable to all working environments. According to the Carl D. Perkins Vocational and Technical Education Act website (http://www.ihdi.uky.edu./kyada/carlperkins.htm) the 1990 Act emphasized two approaches:

(1) Integrating vocational and academic education so that students gain strong basic and advanced academic skills in a vocational setting and (2) Providing students with strong experience in and understanding of all aspects of the industry they are preparing to enter, including planning, management, finance, technical and production skills, underlying principles of technology, labor, community, and health, safety, and environmental issues. (p.1)

This act also addressed the rights of people who were considered to be a part of "special populations" including for example students with disabilities, the disadvantaged, single parents, and people with limited English proficiency. It was made very clear in this legislation that there should be equal access to services and that discrimination would not be tolerated within the structure of this act.

In addition, according to the act, it was the responsibility of the local districts who were receiving the funding to develop specific guidelines as to what their plan was going to entail. They were also to be responsible for overseeing the fact that funds were being distributed equitably. This should have been done through a variety of programs and experiences. In 1998, the Perkins Act was amended because some of the demands it made were beyond the reach of the funding available in many states. As of 2004, almost every school district and community college in the United States receives Perkins funds.

The next legislation to affect the school-to-career movement is the School-to-Work Opportunities Act of 1994 (STWOA). "The roots of the School-to-Work Opportunities Act can be found in the work of two influential policy commissions: the Secretary's Commission on Achieving Necessary Skills (SCANS) and the Commission on the Skills of the American Workforce (CSAW). Both commissions comprised of prominent corporate, labor, and educational leaders." (Levine, 1994, p. 35) According to the U.S. Department of Labor Employment and Training Administration website, STWOA made available $1,270,000 per year to award grants for programs that served youth with both the "out-of-school" and "school-to-work" frameworks. The grant awards ranged from $75,000 to $150,000 and were to be used over a 5-year period.

In order to be awarded a STWOA grant, the system had to have school-based learning opportunities, work-based learning components and connecting activities components. This ties in clearly with the federal beliefs that "STWOA was not a programmatic effort, but a *systems-building strategy* designed to support and extend state and local education reform as well as workforce and economic development efforts." (Brand & Partee, 2001, p.iii) Brand & Partee (2001) emphasize that STWOA has ten Essential Principles. They fall under the headings of Improving the School Experience, Expanding and Improving Work-Based Learning Opportunities, and Building and Sustaining Public/Private Partnerships. These principals are: (1) promote high standards of academic learning and performance for all young people, (2) incorporate industry-valued standards that help inform curricula and lead to respected and portable credentials, (3) provide opportunities for contextual learning, (4) help to create smaller, more effective learning communities, (5) expand opportunities for all young people and expose them to a broad array of career opportunities, (6) provide program continuity between K-12 and postsecondary education and training, (7) provide work-based learning that is directly tied to classroom learning, (8) assist employers in providing high quality work-based learning opportunities (9) connect young people with supportive adults, mentors and other role models and (10) promote the role of brokering/intermediary organizations.

Brand and Partee (2001) explain that "this [was a] one-time, venture capital initiative to help states and localities support the initial costs of planning and establishing statewide systems." (p. 1) Upon passage of this act, it was assumed that there would be no need to continue it after the five year time period because the essential purpose was to set up programs and lay the foundation and professional development that would enable the programs to continue once the funding was over. STWOA allowed for the states and local districts to apply for and utilize the funds as they deemed appropriate. Whereas the Perkins Act and other legislation such as the Individuals with Disabilities Education Improvement Act (IDEA) focus on vocational opportunities for both "disabled" and "needy" students, what is unique about STWOA is that it was intended to create a system that will be beneficial to *all* students. Incorporated in this is the plan to either find replacement funds or to create programs that will not need funds or be self-sustaining. Unfortunately, this portion of the plan was not contained within the federal legislation that eventually became STWOA.

In 2001, Teachers College, Columbia University released a report of accomplishments since this 1994 legislation. These include: (1) Students demonstrated improved attendance and goals and are less likely to drop out, (2) Participating employers and teachers were generally enthusiastic about STW and believe it is beneficial to themselves, their organizations, and their employers/students, (3) Career Academies that linked corporate involvement to secondary school education and fostered small learning communities are cited as an especially effective model, and (4) There were indications that STW funds have stimulated creation of new systems that will endure. More than half the states have enacted legislation to maintain or expand the initiatives that began with federal funds.

In 1998 an act known as the Workforce Investment Act (WIA), also called PL 105-220, went into effect at the federal level. According to the Workforce Investment Act website (2004), the WIA was designed to

Increase the employment, retention and earnings of participants, and increase occupational skill attainment by participants and as a result, improve the quality of the workforce, reduce welfare dependency, and enhance the productivity and competitiveness of the Nation. (¶ 2)

The intent of WIA was that it made employment services available to adults as well as to youth who were deemed "eligible" for these services. Part of this process included creating a Local Board or a Youth Council in each State which was to address any issues that would deal with procurement of funds as well as any issues that deal with codes of conduct and conflicts of interest. The intent was also that the people who were looking for these services should be able to find them all in one location. This "One-Stop delivery system" provided for a full range of services to assist where needed.

The most recent federal legislation to be passed would be PL 113-128, the Workforce Innovation and Opportunity Act of 2014 (WIOA). According to the United States Department of Labor,

formula funds are provided to states and outlying areas, states in turn provide local workforce areas resources to deliver a comprehensive array of youth services that focus on assisting out-of-school youth and in-school youth with one or more barriers to employment prepare for post-secondary education and employment opportunities, obtain educational and/or skills training credentials and secure employment with career/promotional opportunities (2019).

The United States Department of Labor created a "Stakeholder Agreement" as its promise of collaboration. "The U.S. Department of Labor (DOL), in coordination with federal partners the U.S. Departments of Education (ED) and Health and Human Services (HHS), collaborated to provide information and resources for States, local areas, nonprofits and other guarantees, and other stakeholders to assist with WIOA enactment" (U. S. Department of Labor, 2019).

The most important of these reforms is the $10 billion in annual funding to serve almost 20 million Americans each year. WIOA's "Final Rules" (2016) states that it will serve these people through ensuring accountability for employment results, improving transparency for job seekers to help them make better choices, strengthen employer engagement and service businesses, and enhancing coordination and collaboration across programs.

Chapter 3: Perspectives Regarding School-to-Career

School-to-Career also does not have a singular point of view. It can be identified and examined several ways depending how programs are perceived, the variety of school districts, programs, and differing viewpoints.

Areas across the country are divided into various districts called Education Reference Groups (ERGs). According to the Connecticut State Department of Education's website, an ERG is a "classification of the state's public school districts into groups based on similar socio-economic status and need....Under this scheme, school districts were grouped into nine ERGs based on the characteristics of the families with children in public school" (p. 1). The characteristics that the ERGs are based on include income, education, occupation, poverty, family structure, home language, and district enrollment. The school districts that are within the same ERG all have a similar median of percentages in the aforementioned areas. The viewpoints that a district or program adopts is unavoidably shaped by its ERG classification. The viewpoints examined here include rural, urban, career-oriented, legislative and those who are opposed to school-to-career.

The following are representative of the various viewpoints throughout the United States. They are meant to act as a sampling of the kinds of issues that arise with the focus of the various views.

The Rural Perspective

The following section will define and discuss the rural point of view toward school-to-career. This is based on interviewing two representatives of rural districts along with investigating scholarly research and documentation from what would be considered rural communities.

According to Harmon (1999),

> *In rural America, creating quality work-based learning opportunities has more to do with understanding students and their families, parent and community involvement, and local community and economic development than with how students must be able to compete in a "global economy." (p. 23)*

Plymouth, Connecticut is one of these rural districts. Lisa Aiudi, former School-to-Career Coordinator for the Town of Plymouth, Connecticut was interviewed as a representative of a rural community. Plymouth is a town in Litchfield County, Connecticut, a rural area of the state. Plymouth considers itself a "small school district" based on information from their Strategic School Profile (SSP). It has a population of 11,634 and an average per capita income of $53,750 per year. The total school enrollment is approximately 1,901 with 95% of those students being

Caucasian.

Plymouth has a very active school-to-career program and it is extremely enmeshed within the town itself. According to Plymouth School-to-Career Mission Statement,

> *School-to-Career is an integral part of the educational process in the Plymouth School District. It offers all students in grades K-12 the opportunity to explore programs relevant to their career goals through work-based, school-based and connecting activities. This initiative includes a direct relationship between businesses, schools and community. The School-to-Career Program works in conjunction with the school community in this effort to prepare all students to be better contributors to the workforce and to become responsible members of society. (Plymouth School-to-Career, 2004)*

This viewpoint shows a distinct reciprocity between the school and the community at large. This helps to unify the town as a whole and is beneficial to all parties involved. According to Mrs. Aiudi, the School-to-Career program in Plymouth is a necessity to the district and town. It ties the students to their futures and gives them another purpose for coming to school. It is important for lifelong learning, and brings everyone together. School-to-career programs help to keep closer ties with all of the students. It therefore brings everyone together and enables the district to make a difference and not "lose" students.

According to Mrs. Aiudi, one of the most important aspects of a rural school-to-career program is that everybody needs to be "on board". There should be a continuum of support from the teachers, to the administration and on to the school board. This support system should emanate from the school system into the community at large so that both the community and the school system could not imagine not having each other there for support. According to Mrs. Aiudi, this is vital for a rural program to be able to survive. It is an integral aspect that the community-at-large, know and understand what school-to-career education is all about. It is important for the students to be directly involved in the community in which they live.

One of the greatest obstacles that a rural school-to-career program encounters is that of finances. Federal funding for school-to-career programs was only available for a limited amount of time, and it was up to the districts themselves to put programs into play that could last far beyond the finances originally provided. Some districts kept this information in mind and used the money for professional development and to create working relationships with business partners in the communities. According to Mrs. Aiudi, these set a foundation that helped keep programs running even after the funding was cut. Unfortunately, there are other districts that did not take this same direction and used the money to fund positions and to obtain short-term items rather than look at "the big picture." Because of the small size of these districts and the limitations on funding many programs were forced out and downsized dramatically. According to Mrs. Aiudi, this is one of the areas where the federal government was not as diligent as they should have been with keeping track of funding and for what purpose the monies were specifically used. Accountability and follow through were lacking, especially in the smaller districts.

It is a belief, particularly in the rural districts, that setting a solid foundation in the school-to-career programs, getting the students involved in the community, and getting the community involved in the school system makes the work easier when it comes time to pass and/or increase budgets and programs. As a matter of fact, the Plymouth School system not only has a thirty-hour community service requirement for high school graduation, but also it states that, "Through a bonding of family, school and community, we will develop a partnership in education, providing an opportunity for high achievement and excellence, while recognizing different learning styles" (Plymouth Public Schools, 2004) as one of its statements in its Commitment in Education Excellence. According to Mrs. Aiudi, School-to-Career is part of a "domino effect" in the community that is helping it to grow stronger as a whole, from the students on up to the senior citizens within the community. Communities, especially rural communities, need to realize that school-to-career opportunities are for all students and not just those who are not planning to go to college. School-to-career programs teach skills that are transferable to a variety of situations in the college arena and life in general.

The Urban Perspective

Two programs were looked at to represent the urban point of view. These are the Governor's Prevention Partnership, which is based in Hartford, Connecticut, and the New Haven Regional Workforce Development Board.

1) Governor's Prevention Partnership

The Governor's Prevention Partnership is an urban-based resource that works with Connecticut students in the communities of Waterbury, Danbury, Branford, Bridgeport, Fairfield County, and Hartford, all of which are considered urban and large communities within the state of Connecticut (50 states.com, 2005). According to the Governor's Prevention Partnership website (2004), the focus of this program is to reduce "risk factors" in students in urban settings in order to help these students be successful. The program is divided into three basic entities. These are: (a) environmental, consisting of support systems in relationships, meaningful activities, and expectations of success; (b) individual, consisting of social competence, interpersonal skills, problem solving skills and autonomy skills; and (c) resiliency, which consists of acts of helpfulness, optimism, interventions, caring connections, and opportunities.

One of the major ways that the Governor's Prevention Partnership accomplishes these goals is through its "School-to-Career Mentoring Research Project." According to an interview with Stephanie Nicholas of the Governor's Prevention Partnership – Career Mentoring Program, this program is based on a Michigan model and began at the conception of the Governor's Prevention Partnership in 1989. Because the urban population is large and inherently consists of many "at risk" students, the focus of such mentoring programs is essentially to develop positive relationships and to give students real world opportunities to explore careers, college planning, etc. The main focus of the entire program including the Career Mentoring Program portion, according to Ms. Nicholas, is to keep kids "safe, healthy, and drug free." According to the Connecticut Mentoring Partnership's website:

> *The mentor develops a working relationship with a student, models appropriate workplace behavior, and coaches the student regarding behaviors, attitudes, and skills. The mentor also helps the student understand the value of each task, how the student's work contributes to or influences the goals of an organization, and how the requirements of the workplace relate to what the student is learning in*

school. (2004, Mentoring page)

This helps create that much needed connection between school and a successful future that many urban students do not often see.

According to the Governor's Prevention Partnership website:

The Governor's Prevention Partnership has joined a collaborative partnership that includes the Department of Mental Health and Addiction services, the Workplace, Inc. (Bridgeport) and the Yale Consultation Center to study the impact of mentoring on fostering school-to-career readiness and reducing substance abuse and other risky behaviors in urban youth to facilitate replication of the project. (Governor's Prevention Partnership, 2004, p. 1)

This statement shows the inherent difficulties that urban programs have over rural programs: The greater incidences of high risk behaviors in the students. Thus, they are a specific focus of their mission statement. The Governor's Prevention Partnership and Ms. Nicholas personally believe that in order to make a student successful, the risky behaviors have to be reduced, enabling them a greater chance of success. This helps to reduce the drop-out rate that is usually higher in urban districts.

With the mentor program at the hub of the Governor's Prevention Partnership's dropout prevention program, according to Ms. Nicholas, there is a need for more empirical data to show if the Governor's Prevention Partnership has actually helped at risk students to have success. Ms. Nicholas considers most of the data at this time is anecdotal. People seem to "know" or "believe" that the program is helping students but there needs to be more proof. Unfortunately, it is often that way with urban programs. Many students are difficult to "track" and because of the great numbers, follow through is often extremely difficult.

2) New Haven Regional Workforce Development Board

New Haven is a city in New Haven County in southern Connecticut. According to the 2003 Strategic School Profile, New Haven has a population of 123,626 and a mean income of $16,393. Over 66% of the students qualify for free or reduced lunch and over 29% do not speak English at home. There is a higher transient rate compared to rural areas. Over 89% of the students in this district are minority students. It is easy to see that these figures are quite different from those in a rural community. These students are also more likely to participate in "at risk" behaviors and need to be shown the connections between their education and their futures.

According to an interview with Michael Mongillo, the urban districts are the districts that truly need school-to-career programs. Mr. Mongillo advocates that with the No Child Left Behind legislation, districts are going to be more concerned with standardized testing and exit criteria tests than ever before. School-to-career programs can help them with this. It gives the students a tie-in between their schooling and their futures. It gives them a greater purpose for coming to school. Mr. Mongillo believes this purpose will help increase attendance. If these students are in the classroom more often, they will "absorb" more of the information that is being taught; therefore, it is a logical consequence of this that they will do better on these important state tests.

In addition, according to the interview with Mr. Mongillo, "School-to-Career" as an entity has changed quite a lot over the last several years from what was traditionally considered "vocational education". The original term and programs were geared more for "on the job training" and training students for a "job". More recently, these programs, which have moved to using the term "school-to-career" along with "school-to-work" for the same reason (see Appendix B), are focused on life long skills that can transfer into any career as well as into any college situation such as interviewing skills, interpersonal skills, etiquette, and being on time and responsible. That is what the youth in the urban areas need to give them an "edge" in an extremely competitive world:

> *Regardless of the path they take, the ultimate goal of every student is to become a successful, productive member of society....Successful School-to-Career Initiatives can help students make the connection between education and work, and provide them with a solid foundation for making valid education and career choices (New Haven Public Schools, 1998)*

According to the New Haven Area Initiative for School-to-Work Opportunities 1994 grant application, New Haven has one of the highest drop-out rates in Connecticut. Also according to this grant application, the goal of the New Haven Regional Workforce Development Board (1994) is to create a quality system that is "accessible and appealing to students, responsive to the needs of the private sector, easily aligned with a developing statewide system, expandable to serve all interested students within each district and replicable" (p. i). The community sector is tapped for the purpose of providing placement for the various internship and externship opportunities that the program makes available in order to assist its students.

It is relatively easy to see the stark contrast between the rural-based programs and the urban-based programs, even within a relatively small state such as Connecticut. Rural programs are focused more on creating a sense of "community" and volunteerism as part of their day-to-day activities in their school-to-career programs. Urban programs are more focused on improving the chances of the students to have successful futures through the use of drop-out prevention programs and through programs that help students find alternatives to participating in at-risk behaviors commonly associated with a more urban community.

The Career-Oriented Perspective

A "career-oriented" program refers to a program that is not traditionally in the "public schools" arena. These types of programs are those that are already considered focused on careers.

According to the Connecticut Regional-Technical School System's website:

The State of Connecticut funds and operates the Connecticut Regional Vocational-Technical School System, a statewide system of eighteen regional vocational-technical schools and two satellite programs serving approximately 10,000 full-time high school students and approximately 5,500 mostly part-time adult students, with comprehensive education and training in 37 occupational areas. (2004, p.2)

Vocational-Technical system students include, over 41% minority and over 36% free or reduced lunch. These students not only receive a high school diploma upon graduation, but they also receive a certificate stating that they have received training in a specific occupation. According to the mission statement of the Connecticut Regional Vocational-Technical School System, they are dedicated to providing "a rigorous educational program meeting the needs of Connecticut's citizens and employers through academic instruction, intensive occupation-specific training, and apprenticeship credit" (Connecticut State Board of Education, 2004, p. 3). There can be issues where vocational-technical high schools within the same state do not have a standard curriculum. There is a national trend to address this as well as to standardize both exit and entrance criteria for these systems.

Vocational-technical school systems offer certifications in many fields including: auto body repair, automotive mechanics, aviation mechanics, baking, bioscience environment technology, building and remodeling, carpentry, culinary arts, dental assistant, dental laboratory technician, digital microprocessor technician, drafting-architectural, drafting-machine, early childhood career, electrical, electromechanical, electronics, engine repair-diesel, fashion technology, graphic communications, hairdressing/cosmetology/barbering, health technology, heating/ventilation/air conditioning, home health aide/certified nurse assistant, hotel/hospitality technology, information and supportive services, interactive media, manufacturing technology, masonry, medical assistant, metal trades technology, microcomputer software technician, network systems, plumbing and heating, practical nurse education, programming and software development, signal and communication, surgical technician, welding, etc.

While on the surface, vocational-technical schools look as though they are strictly focused on career preparation, this is not necessarily so. According to the Connecticut Vocational-Technical School System's brochure titled *Where Careers Begin* (2002), "more than 30% of its graduating seniors go on to further education; many have been accepted at colleges and universities throughout the United States" (Question and Answer section). When used in conjunction with a college that participates in a "Tech Prep" program, students can earn up to 14 college credits while attending a vocational-technical high school.

Technical-vocational schools traditionally take on a "rotation system". Students will take "academic" classes for a segment of time and then take their "shop" classes for the same segment of time. The freshmen participate in an exploratory program where they spend time in each shop that is available at that particular school in order to get an understanding for what is required of that shop. After completing this exploratory program, students choose the shop that they are going to be focusing on for the remainder of their time at the school. This helps the students to concentrate on what they are truly interested in and want to pursue as a career, giving students a purpose to come to school on a regular basis. This is demonstrated in the Strategic School Profile by the low dropout rate of only 1.2% as compared to a state average of 2.1%. They are now focusing on more "well-rounded" students who would work well in the type of environment that the school provides. In the past, vocational-technical schools had a bad reputation as a place for students to go who would not have the ability or desire to go to college. The new requirements will help in changing that reputation. The requirements for admission are based on test scores, attendance, behavioral records, and an interview.

The graduation requirements are becoming more structured in vocational schools as well. According to the Technical High Schools Program of Studies (2004, p. 5), beginning with the Class of 2008, (students who are freshmen in 2004) students need a total of 28½ credits in order to graduate. Nine of them are part of the Technology Program; three are from the Exploratory Program. There are a total of 13 in academics (English-4; Social Studies-3; Mathematics-3; Science-3). Other requirements complete the credits (Physical Education-1; Health-1/2; Electives-2). It is believed that the biggest stumbling block students from the vocational-technical school system have getting accepted to and attending college is that there are usually no foreign language classes available within these systems. What most students do is attend a community college to earn these credits and then transfer to a college or university.

The Career High Schools Perspective

Career high schools are interdistrict magnet schools that encompass regional areas within a state. These types of schools have been around for quite some time but are beginning to "come into their own". These students are taught transferable skills that they could use in any career situation. They are involved with job shadowing, on-site visits, internships, and keeping a journal.

In an interview with Mr. Charles Wiliams, principal of one such school, he states that the best thing to come out of the school-to-career initiatives is that it was the onset of the recognition that many students may opt not to further their education. School-to-career makes it viable to find substantial income for those students. The school itself boasts that over 90% of its graduates go on to higher education. In addition, over 20% of its juniors and seniors are enrolled in courses for college credit.

According to the profile:

Suburban students attend Career for its high curricular standards, instruction, partnerships, student achievement and extra-curricular opportunities and records in addition to the school's theme focus on careers in either health/science or business/ computers. (p. 2)

This focus is emphasized through its community relationships with local companies, colleges, and universities. Examples of this include students in the Anatomy and Physiology courses and Advanced Biology courses. They spend one day a week studying at Yale University alongside medical students. Nursing students work with faculty and students at Southern Connecticut State University.

They emphasize skills and practices that will lead toward a specific career goal. This is different from the public school systems, which put more of their focus on academics and often treat school-to-career programs as secondary to what students need. This is a way of thinking that advocates of school-to-career systems are trying to change. Proponents of school-to-career programs attempt to show that the skills and strategies taught in school-to-career classes and programs and those taught at career-oriented schools are transferable to countless situations that students may encounter in their lifetimes. Edutopia in their meta analysis of school-to-career reports show that

> *Career Academies ...increase both the levels of interpersonal [support] students [experience] during high school and their participation in career awareness and work-based learning activities; Career academies substantially [improve] high school outcomes among students at risk of dropping out; and Academies [reduce] dropout rates, [improve] attendance, [increase] academic course taking and [increase] the likelihood of earning enough credits to graduate on time (2021).*

The Tech Prep Perspective

Tech Prep is a system that has its base in the community college system. The Tech Prep system is one that works in cooperation with school districts, especially those with a "high risk" population. They work with districts to try to connect them to local businesses and they work with students to keep them from having an "isolated" view of what careers are. They try to give both teachers and students an expanded view of what the reality of a career is; they work with teachers to educate them on how to tie in the subject matter to the workplace and future careers rather than just teaching a subject for the subject's sake.

Tech Prep tries to work within the school systems to get students pointed in the right direction. It assists students with applications and even prerequisite fulfillment for attending the local community colleges. This is done with the hopes that the students will not only complete their degrees at the community college but also continue their education at a local college or university.

The Perspectives Against School-to-Career

Not all constituents feel that school-to-career programs are good for all students. In fact, there is a very strong opposition to school-to-career programs not only in Connecticut, but also across the United States. The Eagle Forum is one of the strongest opponents of school-to-career legislation in the United States and will be the focus of examination in this section.

The Eagle Forum is an organization that has existed since 1967. The president of this organization since its conception is Phyllis Schlafly. According to the Eagle Forum's Mission Statement, its mission is to:

> *Enable conservative and pro-family men and women to participate in the process of self-government and public policy-making so that America will continue to be a land of individual liberty, respect for family integrity, public and private virtue, and private enterprise.*

What began as a "grassroots" effort has grown into a national organization based in Alton, Illinois.

The Eagle Forum has spoken out against school-to-career initiatives often. This was especially true between 1995 and 1997, when most of the initiatives were beginning to take root. In 1995, the first of a series of articles was written by Mrs. Schlafly against school-to-career legislation. She states that the School-to-Work Opportunities Act (STWOA) of 1994 was "one of the worst Clinton bills passed [in 1994]" (Schlafly, 1995, ¶ 2). In this document, Mrs. Schlafly goes on to criticize Marc Tucker, president of the National Center on Education and the Economy for being an impetus behind STWOA. She cites Tucker as supporting:

A system of labor market boards [to be] established at the local, state, and federal levels to coordinate the systems for job training, postsecondary professional and technical education, adult basic education, job matching and counseling. (Schlafly, 1995, ¶ 7)

This is the type of initiative against which the Eagle Forum is fighting. Mrs. Schlafly states that "Tucker's plan would change the mission of the public schools from teaching children knowledge and skills to training then to serve the global economy in jobs selected by workforce boards" (Schlafly, 1997a, p. 1). The members of the Eagle Forum believe that:

The traditional function of education was to teach basic knowledge and skills: reading, writing, math, science, history, etc. School-to-Work deemphasizes or eliminates academic work and substitutes mandated vocational training to serve the workforce. Instead of the focus being on developing the child, the focus is on serving the labor force. (Schlafly, 1997a, p. 2)

This viewpoint is in contradiction to the very spirit with which STWOA was written. The lawmakers, along with President Clinton, were trying to create a system in which students would be able to explore opportunities and learn transferable skills that will assist them in making choices for their futures. The Eagle Forum believes that the "real goal of the Clinton Administration's plan is to eliminate local control of public schools" (Schlafly, 1997a, p. 3). Even if they agreed with the school-to-career legislation, they still believe that "it's not the job of the taxpayers to do job training; that's the job of corporations that hire them. It is the job of the schools to teach children to read, write, and calculate" (Schlafly, 1997a, p. 2). They advocate that School-to-Work is not a fad, that it is a "systematic change in the school's mission, the curriculum, and its lasting effect on students" (Schlafly, 1997b, p. 1).

Another concern that the Eagle Forum has is that School-to-Work legislation will change the focus of education to a "training" system rather than a system that educates and teaches. They even make that point very clear on the cover of one of their brochures titled *Will your child be educated or trained in 'School-to-Work'?* (1997). Next to the word "educated" there are two graduates with their caps and gowns on and diplomas in their hands. Next to the word "trained" is a picture of a dog jumping through a hoop. Mrs. Schlafly explains that there is quite a difference between the two terms. She states that "to educate means to develop the faculties and powers of a person by teaching" (Schlafly, 1997b, p. 1) and that "to train means to cause a person or animal to be efficient in the performance of tasks by responding to discipline, instruction, and repeated practice." (Schlafly, 1997b, p. 1) The Eagle Forum sees School-to-Work legislation as "a direct threat to the individual student, his privacy, his goals, and his acquisition of an education that can help him reach these goals. It's also a direct threat to freedom as we know it in America" (Schlafly, 1997b, p. 2).

In this brochure, the Eagle Forum informs the reader that there are a variety of education innovations directly connected to school-to-career programs that they believe are integral in the downfall of the education system in America. Ironically, these are the very concepts that teachers and education leaders are learning about, promoting, and advocating. According to the brochure these innovations include: (a) self esteem, which the Eagle Forum translates to students being taught to "feel good" rather than to read; (b) outcome based education and cooperative learning, in which Eagle Forum believes that students are encouraged to stick with the mediocrity rather than to excel; (c) diversity and tolerance, which Eagle Forum believes that all behaviors and lifestyles are acceptable; (d) multiculturalism, which Eagle Forum believes teaches students that America is bad and oppressive; (e) values clarification and decision making, which Eagle Forum believes encourages students to make decisions without adult direction; (f) critical thinking which Eagle Forum states criticizes parents' morals and religion; (g) whole language in which Eagle Forum believes that educators teach students to guess at words and skip over what they don't know; (h) inventive spelling, by which Eagle Forum believes that children are told that it is OK to spell any way they want; (i) school based clinics in which a school provides medical care; and (j) guidance which Eagle Forum members argue encourages students to confide in virtual strangers rather than parents. They believe that "Americans do not want their children to be pawns in this giant and expensive experiment" (Eagle Forum, 1997, p. 3) and that when students are educated in the basic skills that all other aspects of their lives will fall naturally into place.

The Eagle Forum is definitely strong in their voice concerning the issues that they are in agreement with and to which they are opposed. As a matter of fact in their brochure that "invites" people to "build a better educated, safer, stronger America based on traditional values," (Eagle Forum, cover) they state "We opposed federal control of the public school classroom through Goals 2000, School-to-Work, national tests or national standards" (Eagle Forum, p. 3). They have a nationwide network of similar-minded people and fight vehemently for their goals. Through this network, people opposed the school-to-career initiatives write letters and have meetings to voice their concerns. The Eagle Forum and Phyllis Schlafly still work hard today, a decade later, to enlarge their network and to "prove that citizen-volunteers can affect government policies in Congress, state legislatures, city councils, and school boards; elect candidates at every level; and articulate conservative and pro-family policies through the media" (Eagle Forum, p. 5).

We have seen that one's viewpoint of school-to-career programs and their importance depends on what your place is both geographically and morally.

Chapter 4: Interview Results

Interviews were conducted with several stakeholders in the School-to-Career arena. These included a state representative, principal of a career focused high school, a director of Area Cooperative Educational Services, a School-to-Career coordinator, a representative from the Career and Technical Education School System, a School-to-Career Tech Prep coordinator, a representative from The Governor's Prevention Partnership Career Mentor Program, the Vice-President of the Connecticut Business and Industry Association, and an assistant superintendent for the State of Connecticut Department of Education.

The majority of those interviewed felt that one of the best things to come out of the school-to-career movement is the local partnerships and relationships that were formed. They reported that these relationships were important for a variety of reasons. These ranged from reasons of visibility within the community to building a sense of community. According to the interviews, there is perceived reciprocity between a school system and a community, and the ensuing working relationship is seen as mutually beneficial. Another common response was educators seeing the creation of opportunities for students to develop skills that they will need in their future careers. These are done by the school systems for the students. There appears to be a consensus among those interviewed that these opportunities create a link between the school and the futures of the students participating in the various school-to-career programs. Those interviewed believe that this connection helps to give the students a purpose for going to school and helps to decrease dropout rates.

A common regret about the school-to-career movement is that the federal limitations on both time and money were too restrictive. The respondents felt that a five-year window did not allow enough time to design, plan, initiate, and fully implement worthwhile and lasting programs. Programs were started but when the federal funds ran out and the budgets were getting tighter, these programs took a "back seat" to other programs that the schools felt were more important. Specifically discussed was the need for more agencies to work together more to make professional development available statewide. This should also include more involvement of school counselors and a career guidance system to help create links between the students and their lives upon exiting school in order to help keep them motivated.

It is significant to note here that this response is very different from the responses to other questions. It crossed various viewpoints and groupings. While there were other responses that tapped into other issues, the issues of time and money stand out as a concern of many.

The overwhelming majority of those interviewed stated that they believed that school-to-career should be a part of every school's curriculum. The most common reason given was that it created a tie between school and the futures of the students. Several also believe that this tie creates a purpose for coming to school and, therefore, will increase attendance and scores. While this line of reasoning is debatable by some in that opponents of school-to-career initiatives do not feel that such a connection is made, those that expressed it were adamant and passionate about it.

Finally, when those interviewed were asked a very open-ended question regarding any thoughts that they feel they would like to convey, the issue of the cut of the federal funding came into play again. This was a strong theme throughout these interviews. It is a theme that not only spanned the variety of people interviewed, but it also crossed questions showing up as answers and/or as a follow up to a number of the questions asked.

Although the intent of the interviews was to gain a variety of perspectives regarding school-to-career, a limitation to this study is that, in the attempt to be well rounded, the people that were interviewed, by the very nature of the positions that they hold, were biased toward the school-to-career initiatives. They are each a stakeholder in their own right. They came across as believing in the concepts and ideals of school-to-career programs. Because of this limitation, it is important that when interpreting the data that the reader realizes that the data itself has the potential to be skewed in that direction.

This information, although derived from anecdotal sources, plays an important role in creating the whole picture with regard to school-to-career programs. A very important part of that picture is that there were shortcomings within programs.

In addition to looking at school-to-career's past, it is important to investigate its present as well. This could be done by surveying districts that still actively participate in school-to-career programs. The programs that are in existence currently could be investigated. Districts could then work collaboratively to determine which programs have been successful and which ones are continuing to be a part of that system. This could create a common collection of successful, cost-effective ideas.

This would then tie into a further topic of research for the future. What are districts' plans for the future transitions of their students? How are these going to be carried out even though there is no more federal funding that exists for them?

If what educators believe about school-to-career programs is true, then they truly still need to be a part of a district's curriculum. This being so, how school-to-career relates to other school curriculums in general is a matter that needs to be considered in any future revision of *The Common Core of Learning*.

Chapter 5: Analysis and Critique

It is important to stand back and reflect objectively on the developments that have taken place. When reviewing the data and history, one can find that there are several themes that emerge. These themes include money, time, accountability, standardization, inclusion of all students, and the creation of a "plan".

Money and Time

A common thread running through most of the school-to-career literature is that of money and the fact that money and time are linked together as a school-to-career issue. This dates back to the Smith-Hughes Act of 1917 when the federal government first allocated money for school-to-work efforts. This funding was to go toward programs to assist students who were not planning to attend college to prepare for their roles in society. Money was controversial with this act because the focus of this act was on the education of females for the purpose of home economics. Even in the *Cardinal Principles of Secondary Education*, time is addressed in the statement that "Education must be conceived as a process of growth. Only when so conceived and so conducted can it become a preparation for life" (§VII, ¶1). The concern of funding and time is echoed through other legislative acts including the more recent Carl D. Perkins Vocational Education Act of 1990 and the School-to-Work Opportunities Act of 1994 (STWOA). According to Hughes, Bailey, & Karp (2002) "the authors of STWOA had not intended to create a permanent separate 'program.' Rather, their goal was to generate activities that could then be incorporated to the normal functioning of the education system" (p. 272). This point is argued as the reason why there was a limit on the federal funding of STWOA (Hughes, Bailey, & Karp, 2002). Money, time, or both were mentioned as an issue of some sort in every interview conducted, including the fact that 50% of those interviewed specifically mentioned that the limits of time and too little money given by the federal government was too short. The National Conference of State Legislatures' website mentions the fact that many districts were trying to find ways to continue this reform effort even though the School-to-Work Act was in its "sunset." This left many school systems scrambling to find ways to continue the school reform even though the funding was running out, by trying to align existing funding with school-to-career efforts.

Nowadays, there is the realization that "educational reform is much more complex than anticipated" (Fullan, 2001, p. 17). According to the work of Daniel Duke (2004), educational change is a process, not an event. The first proposition of his model of educational change states, "Educational change tends to occur over time and involve predictable activities" (Duke, 2004, p. 253). Many leaders in the field of educational change (Bolman & Deal, 1997; Danielson, 2002; Duke, 2004; Fullan, 2001) believe that the change process within any organization takes time to implement. When creating and developing school-to-career plans, according to Fouad (1997), one must "be prepared to play a role in systematic change, understanding it as well as responses to the change process....It is critical to understand the forces that operate when entire systems change, with external and internal pressures by some to change and others to remain the same" (p. 411). Research by Charner, Macallum, & White (1999) support the fact that changes cannot be made overnight. It takes time to begin to see results. Charner, Macallum, & White (1999) do, however, believe that "while it is important to recognize that any school reform effort is unlikely to have an immediate impact on student performance, longer-range evaluations should have a noticeable effect on attendance, grades, course selection, student performance, graduation rates, and future planning" (p. 10). Writing of the eleven basic assumptions of a successful approach to educational change, Fullan (2001) says:

> *Assume that effective change takes time. It is a process of "development in use." Unrealistic or unidentified time lines fail to recognize that implementation occurs developmentally. Significant change in the form of implementing specific innovations can be expected to take a minimum of 2 to 3 years; bringing about institutional reforms can take 5 to 10 years. At the same time, work on changing infrastructure. (p. 109)*

Even though this theory about time needed for successful educational change has come to the forefront more recently in educational reform, school-to-career advocates have known this for quite some time. An example is the work of McKinnon and Jones (1975) in Mesa, Arizona. Their whole plan was based on the fact that the change was going to be a process and not a panacea. Their work with the Mesa schools took from 1972 to 1974 to implement with specific grade levels and was eventually continued to include all of the grades levels by 1977.

According to Hughes, Bailey & Karp (2002):

> *To many, it is [the] goal of system building that differentiates the STWOA from other education or work force development initiatives. States were to use the short-term federal funding to amend or incorporate their existing career preparation activities and to create links between school reform and workforce development efforts. Once the federal appropriation was distributed, the new systems were to be supported by other long-standing education and workforce development funding streams. (p. 273)*

The very fact that STWOA created a monetary limit and a five-year time limit goes against these theories. In referencing the work of Fullan (2001), it is easy to see that an institutional reform of the magnitude of school-to-career reforms needs a minimum of five years to begin to see results. Since that was the maximum time that the STWOA legislation gave funding for reforms, it is almost as if they were destined to fail from the start. This issued is also raised when Fullan (2001) discusses the fact that "*change is a process, not an event* – a lesson learned the hard way by those who put all their energies into developing an innovation or passing a piece of legislation without thinking what would have to happen beyond that point" (p. 52). It appears that, with the five-year time limit and funding limit, the creators, legislators, and implementers of the school-to-career legislation did not have this in the forefront of their thinking when those limits were discussed.

The federal government's time allotment of five years was much too short to allow for the start-up, organization, delivery, assessment, and retooling that the districts needed in order to create and implement a successful school-to-career program. Because of the limited amount of time and the limits on the federal funding, it was and is up to the school districts to set up programs that would last far beyond the finances and to implement those programs. Many towns did not do this and used funds to pay for positions rather than to create long-lasting programs that would go beyond the funding and time limitations.

Fifty percent of those interviewed agree that there were time and money constraints and that many school systems didn't utilize the funding to set up a self-sustaining program. School systems needed more time and money to put programs into place. Given a longer time span, more school systems would have more readily shared the valuable resources and connections that they had made. Schools, especially high schools, guarded their contacts very heavily and would not share names and information. This lack of networking was because the school systems wanted to protect their connections because the time and money was so limited that they did not want other systems to tap into the resources that were at their disposal.

Brand & Partee (2001) remind us that the School-to-Work Opportunities Act (STWOA) was a "one time, venture capital initiative to help states and localities support the initial costs of planning and establishing a statewide system" (p. 1). According to Abt Associates Inc. (2003), financing for these programs was indeed lacking. However, many of the eligible districts did not even take advantage of the funds that were available. The federal funding limit was too low and districts were disappointed in the fact that there was no follow through in funding after the five years were up.

The money was there and available and that if systems did what they were supposed to do with it (which was to start up self-sustaining programs) that the financial limitations were workable. That money should have been used to create a collaborative community and to unify school districts. The money should have been used to provide a variety of professional development opportunities for teachers in the districts in order to have students at all levels and in every subject area be able to tie their interests into school-to-career entities.

It is frustrating to learn that as the money began to run out that many of the great programs that were started were lost. Educators need to rise to the higher challenges of connecting school-to-career with the higher academic challenges and to create an understanding of what to do with that knowledge now that there is no more funding to support the cost of these programs. Even though the funding is no longer directly attached, there are still guidelines to follow.

In contrast, even though the time allotment of five years is complete and the funding is no longer available, according to the National Conference of State Legislatures (2004) the outlook for school-to-career reforms is a positive one. The long-term outlook for at least 10 states in the United States is favorable because many of the districts used the federal funding for start-up costs and utilizing the money as part of the year-to-year operating costs of the programs.

Accountability

According to Duke (2004), "two public ideas of different origin can become linked over time. Such has been the case with educational excellence and accountability" (p. 45). Duke also states that "there are three types of problems related to professional practice – lack of accountability, ineffectiveness, and inefficiency" (2004, p. 72). Accountability in school-to-career programs is not a new issue. As a matter of fact, Benson & Blocher (1975) in their early writings regarding school-to-career issues, state that they consider "evaluating processes and outcomes" as one of their nine steps to facilitating change in any human system. Fullan (2001) states that "the combination of accountability and incentives creates results" (p. 224). Also, according to Danielson (2002) "well-designed assessments can inform educators about the degree to which students are meeting state or district content standards" (p. 86). This became a concern with the way that the school-to-career initiatives were carried out.

In relation to school-to-career legislation, Castellano, Stringfield, and Stone (2003), state that the reauthorizations of the Commission on the Skills of the American Workforce, 1990; National Commission on Excellence in Education, 1983; and SCANS, 1991 "encouraged reforms of vocational education to make a clearer transition to post-secondary education, to infuse more academic rigor, to include more work-related experiences, and to make vocational education more accountable" (p. 246).

Accountability appeared to be a concern when the school-to-career initiatives were first created. As a matter of fact, the Office of Workforce Competitiveness was made responsible for creating a committee to "produce, within available appropriations, a report, including a long-range strategic plan, for information technology workforce development, that addresses…workforce and research needs" (State of Connecticut, Public Act No. 00-187, 2000, §28, §§a).

School-to-career as an entity is unique and it would be difficult to evaluate and hold it accountable by more traditional methods, such as standardized testing. Teachers need to hold their students accountable in nontraditional ways and governing bodies need to hold the teachers and the school systems accountable. This could be done by thinking of alternative methods for assessment rather than the more traditional pen and paper tests. Johnson (2000) emphasizes this point when she states that:

Rather than looking to increase student achievement by teaching students more, we need to focus on educating our students differently through a multitude of integrated approaches that will ensure their ability to understand what they are learning, why they are learning it, how they will use it, and what difference it will make in their lives. (p. 273)

Bishop (1992) also makes this emphasis when he stated, "so that schools can be held accountable for the achievement of their students, measurement of student accomplishment must be fair across schools" (p. 16). There was an inconsistency across the nation; this is shown by the lack of data and statistics regarding programs. One exception is the Abt reports of 2001 and 2003, which were concerned with the school-to-career programs within Connecticut and how the individual districts created programs with the funding given. This study, however, was conducted almost a decade after the passing of the School-to-Work Opportunities Act of 1994.

According to Charner, Macallum, and White (1999), whenever a system implements a new program, it should be evaluated utilizing a five-point evaluation. This plan includes observation, reviewing of student records, portfolios, presentations (performance events), and longitudinal follow up.

An exception to this lack of follow-up information is a doctoral field study using the Plymouth School District to evaluate the way that students felt about their school-to-career educational experiences and how these experiences related to their futures (Doughty-Jenkins, 2003). The purpose of the study was to determine if any association existed between students taking a school-to-career program and their views about what their future careers may be. Upon conducting pre- and post-surveys, this study determined that there was an increase in the number of students who saw connections between school-to-career classes and their futures. There was also enough practical significance to encourage educators to pursue school-to-career programs. It is a shortcoming of the school-to-career programs and literature in Connecticut that there aren't more such field studies, and that these studies are not mandatory, especially now that the federal legislation no longer applies.

There should have been more rigorous accountability measures. This is shown when interviewees were asked about their regrets in dealing with school-to-career legislation. Educators should have actually started the foundational aspects of keeping statistics so that a longitudinal study could have been done. There should have been better statistics kept and that the legislature was not focused on school-to-career as they should have been.

Standardization

According to Schmoker (2000) "at the state and local level, it is paramount that we select, and then provide a clear, simple set of standards for every teacher that corresponds richly with the assessments by which we and our communities will judge our progress" (p. 74). When discussing leadership responsibilities, Sanders (2000) states that it is the responsibility of those in leadership positions to report and evaluate programs based on standards including "standards set by model school districts or models based on professional literature" (p. 46).

The school-to-career movement had determined specific goals for students approximately 50 years ago. These goals or "tasks" helped to create a standard by which school-to-career programs could base their activities as well as their results. These tasks, according to Hansen and Tennyson (1975) are as follows:

Tasks for the primary years:

> *Acquire awareness of self*
> *Gain a sense of control over one's life*
> *Identify with workers*
> *Acquire knowledge about workers*
> *Acquire interpersonal skills*
> *Objectify self before others*
> *Gain respect for other people and the work they do*

Tasks for the intermediate years:

Develop a positive self-concept
Acquire the discipline of work
Identify with the concept of work as a valued institution
Increase knowledge about workers
Increase interpersonal skills
Increase objectification of self before others
Value human dignity

Tasks for the junior high years:

Clarify self-concept
Assume responsibility for career planning
Formulate tentative career goals
Acquire knowledge of occupations, work settings and lifestyles
Acquire knowledge of educational and occupational resources
Develop awareness of the decision making process
Acquire sense of independence

Tasks for the senior high school years:

Reality test the self-concept
Develop awareness of preferred lifestyle
Reformulate tentative goals
Increase knowledge of and experience in occupations and work settings
Acquire knowledge of educational and vocational paths
Clarify the decision making process as related to self
Commit oneself with tentativeness within a changing world

Tasks for the post-high years:

Develop interpersonal skills essential to work
Develop information processing skills about self and work
Reintegrate the self
Acquire a sense of community
Commit oneself to the concept of career
Acquire the determination to participate in change
Creatively apply management skills to life roles

Although this work of Hansen and Tennyson can be helpful, the standards are very vague. The activities that are done throughout the various programs should be genuine and activities that they would really encounter in the workplace. These should be done in actual settings in order to make these experiences as close to what the students will face in their employment situations as possible. School-to-career programs are to be based on the four principles set forth by the federal government. These principles are:

(1) integrated school-based and work-based learning that incorporates academic and occupational learning and links between secondary and postsecondary education, (2) the opportunity for participating students to complete a career major, (3) the provision of a work experience in the industry a student is preparing to enter, and (4) equal access for students to a full range of program components and related activities, such as recruitment, enrollment, and placement. (National Conference of State Legislatures Website)

These standards are school experiences, work experiences, and connecting activities.

These activities should not be in danger of becoming a "cookie cutter" approach. School-to-career programs really need to be individualized to the district that is putting the programs in place.

One of the reasons that standardization among the various agencies that dealt with school-to-career programs was and is difficult is that several agencies were not willing to share resources and knowledge for the greater good. Even though there was some direction, this was seen as more of an approach that placed demands on a program rather than having the individualization that the various districts needed.

Inclusion of All Students

When educators discuss the topic of "inclusion" they typically mean the process by which students with special needs are integrated into the classroom. Quite paradoxically, when discussing the topic of "School-to-Career", inclusion means somewhat the opposite. Traditionally, school-to-career programs have been mostly for special needs students and those who probably would not be furthering their education after high school. According to Castellano, Stringfield, & Stone (2003):

Historically, vocational education programs tended to include the students who were at risk of not finishing high school....However, over the last generation, the globalization of the economy has had an increasing impact on work in the United States....The expectation that a young person could get a well-paid job in the plant where his or her father worked [is] no longer a given....The most important changes [in school-to-career programs] were efforts to increase the academic skills of the career and technical education (CTE) students, erase the stigma sometimes attached to vocational education, and see that all students met the higher standards that had become prevalent. The goal of CTE became for all students to finish high school prepared either to enter the workplace or to begin postsecondary education. This broader mission challenged vocational educators to teach beyond the confines of specific occupations and, instead, to prepare students for a more demanding world of work. (pp. 243-244)

James B. Conant, another pioneer in career education, believed that vocational education should be part of every high school's curriculum and not be limited to being a part of the curriculum of vocational schools (Tozer, Violas, & Senese, 2002). According to Tozer, Violas, &

Senese (2002) "Conant clearly argued that such a separation was inadvisable and that a comprehensive high school should offer different kinds of curricula under the same roof" (p. 331).

According to Duke (2004), "since the early eighties, educational excellence has been associated with two basic beliefs: (a) *all* students need to receive rigorous academic instruction, regardless of their future plans and (b) standards in academic subjects need to be raised significantly" (pp. 43-44). All the students can benefit from the experiences that school-to-career programs provide and these experiences help them to better focus on what they would like to do as a career after they have finished their education. This has come to the forefront with the passage of the No Child Left Behind Act (NCLB) of 2001, which was signed into law on January 8, 2002. Parents and the community-at-large are becoming knowledgeable as to what is going on within the school buildings and are expecting programs to include *all* students.

The viewpoint of including all students is supported by the National Conference of State Legislatures website (2004). It states that one of the major components of school-based learning is "a program of study that meets the academic standards the state has established for *all* students, including where applicable, standards established under the Goals 2000 Act, and meets the requirements of postsecondary education preparation" (§2, ¶5) (emphasis added).

When discussing their "Career Management Model", Hansen & Tennyson (1975) suggested that educators working with students in school-to-career programs keep in mind that "each person has the potential for success and satisfaction in a number of occupations – [this] frees individuals from the fear of making wrong choices and increases their available options" (p. 641). Burke (2004) discusses how educators need to rethink their roles. He also believes that there are expectations for every student when it comes to school-to-career programs. These eight expectations are: (a) the application of what is learned in high school can help a student be successful in their future; (b) college is a means to an end – not the end to learning; (c) education is a lifelong endeavor; (d) it is just as important to experience what they don't want to do as well as what they enjoy doing; (e) each student will have at least three different jobs in their lifetime, some of which may not even be a career in today's world; (f) the computer is a tool and technological literacy is a lifelong skill; (g) the ability to access information and make informed decisions is a required skill; and (h) the ability to see themselves in their future is their best road map to success.

Action Plan

The final theme that permeates the interviews is the creation (or lack thereof) of a specific action plan to keep everyone doing similar activities with regard to school-to-career issues. The national legislation did not have an actual action plan.

Having an action plan helps to keep track of relevant data. According to Schmoker (2000), in order for teams to be truly effective, they should consider "(1) consistency with what we know from pertinent research and (2) our sense of its potential impact on student learning" (p. 16). In order to implement successful programs, we need to be aware of these issues. It would be extremely ineffective to just put together programs that are solely based on a hunch.

According to Charner, Macallum, & White (1999), "to begin, a school needs to examine the goals and objectives of its school-to-career activities. Evaluation and program design must be inextricably linked" (p. 10). Even the earlier school-to-career works of Benson & Blocher (1975) call for a comprehensive plan before beginning a school-to-career program and/or activities. They state that:

Implementing career development programs requires a focus of effort and a precision in planning. In activities that involve the time and energy of many people and cut across many disciplines and personnel, it is essential that a base of demonstrated success be established to provide credibility for future programs. (p. 660)

In addition, similar research during the mid to late 1970s done by Gysbers & Moore (1975) concurs with this viewpoint. Their research states that because society has changed and continues to change, it is important to make school-to-career programs ever changing yet structured in order to keep up with the times. It was during the 1980s that three basic goals of the career education movement came into play. These goals were identified as

(a) to change the educational system by inserting a "careers" emphasis throughout curriculum; (b) to make career education a joint effort with the community, rather than an effort of the educational system alone; and (c) to provide students with a set of general skills for adjusting to the changes in this occupational society (Evans & Burck, 1992, p. 63).

As with any well thought out action plan, there needs to be an opportunity for evaluation and adjustment of what is going on within the programs. Bishop (1992) argues that this evaluation should not be internal, it should be looked at by an external source. He believes that an external source can be more objective. He states that this should carry over from school-to-career to other classes as well. Up until now, we have traditionally looked at individual student achievement as a measure of success. Bishop submits that "external assessment would change this because it turns academic coursework into a positive situation where everyone wins" (p. 17). According to Bolman & Deal (1997) "an organization without a plan is thought to be reactive, shortsighted, and rudderless" (p. 242). They also discuss the relevancy of plans in that they are symbolic, game-like, excuses for interaction and "advertisements" for what is expected. They believe that there is such an importance to having a plan that when they discuss each of their four frameworks of organizational process, they put "strategic planning" as the first topic in each discussion.

According to the work of Bridges (1991), some generalities should be involved with a plan. He submits that these generalities of all plans include an outline of steps and a schedule in which people will receive the information, training, and support that they need, and that lays out the nature and timing of key events.

Miller and Benjamin (1975) are early researchers in the area of the inclusion of a plan in school-to-career programs. They believe that the plan for school-to-career programs involves four basic steps. These are: (a) needs assessment, (b) development of goals and objectives, (c) identification and selection of guidance strategies, and (d) program evaluation. Fullen (2001) gives a list of ten "do" and "don't" assumptions for educational change. In his eighth assumption, he emphasizes the need for a plan. He says that this plan should address all known factors that may affect implementation. This coincides with Miller and Benjamin. Burke (2004) shows educators a more comprehensive plan to put in place for school-to-career programs. The six steps in this plan are (a) recognize the need for school-wide change, (b) involve the community, (c) build staff capacity, (d) identify appropriate career themes and challenges, (e) develop advisory boards around the career themes, and (f) focus on professional development.

Guidelines were originally based on the School-to-Work Opportunities Act of 1994 (STWOA). STWOA "was not a programmatic effort, but a *systems-building strategy* designed to support and extend state and local education reform as well as workforce and economic development efforts" (Brand, Partee, Kaufmann, & Wills, 2000, p. ii). As Levine points out, "the Act is designed to construct a national school-to-work transition system which is administered on the state and local levels, but welded together by commonly-held standards established by the Goals 2000: Educate America Act" (p. 35). The roots of this stem from the Secretary's Commission on Achieving Necessary Skills (SCANS). SCANS was made up of corporate leaders, labor leaders, and leaders in education.

Districts tried to follow the guidelines set by Burke as well as those set by STWOA. This was done through the creation of the career cluster system. The career cluster system took possible careers and clustered them by similarities into clusters: (a) arts and media; (b) business and finance; (c) construction: technologies and design; (d) environmental, natural resources, and agriculture; (e) government, education and human resources; (f) health and biosciences; (g) information technology; (h) retail, tourism, recreation, and entrepreneurship; and (i) technologies: manufacturing, communications and repair (CBIA website, 2004). It would be important to note that the United States now has 16 career clusters, as mentioned in a previous chapter.

Although these clusters gave those responsible for creating a school-to-career curriculum a guideline to follow, districts lack a specific curriculum or even a development guide. The guidelines are considered by some to be a plan for implementation of STWOA. Those responsible for carrying out the programs in need more specific guidelines to follow in order to create action plans for their individual districts.

Chapter 6: The Future

Given what we know of the past, where does this put us for the future? The future of School-to-Career can be a very exciting adventure. There are many new careers developing with artificial intelligence, robotics, etc.

> *Research and practice have led to consensus on the different dimensions of readiness all students need for college and future careers. These include academic mastery across a range of subjects, technical training either in a specific field or in cross-cutting skills such as computer literacy, and 21st-century skills such as critical thinking and collaboration. Most states include these in their definitions of college, career, and life readiness, and some elements of these definitions are included in states' school accountability systems (Jiminez, 2020).*

This is echoed in the United States Department of Labor when they state

> *The bipartisan WIOA [Workforce Innovation Opportunities Act] ...created a new vision for how America prepares an educated and skilled workforce that expands opportunity for workers and employers. The 21st century public workforce system created through WIOA builds closer ties between leaders, State and Local Workforce Development Boards, labor unions, community colleges, non-profit organizations, youth serving organizations, and State and local officials to deliver a more job-driven approach to training and skills development (2019).*

This is to be done through coordinated planning, aligning accountability, and improving service delivery.

It is important for the future generations that,

> *Educators and employers together must identify what systemic changes will result in the development of seamless pathways from education to training, and to good jobs of the future. They will likely need to measure the benchmarks discussed earlier such as early career preparation and holistic readiness. To address historic opportunity gaps, they will also need to measure how they use their resources to close such gaps both to improve the return on investment and to advocate for additional resources from local, state, and federal funding sources (Jiminez, 2020).*

According to Poth (2019) there are 5 conditions for creating an innovative workplace. The conditions are: Dedicating time for creative projects, Rewarding innovation and divergent ideas, Empowering employees to make decisions, Allowing for failure, and Measuring what matters most. These are important skills that need to be focused on during the educational process.

The interesting item to note is that although this may be where the future lies, there is not necessarily a need for college to succeed. According to an August 2019 podcast with WorkIt! founder and CEO, Lori Theriault, titled *"Do I Need to go to College"*, the pendulum is swinging back when it comes to careers and employment. This is a time when a lot of the people who are in the skilled trades are reaching retirement age. This is leaving gaps in this area because so much of the past decades have been dedicated to preparing students for college and not focusing on other avenues. There are employers now who will take people with little to no experience and educate and train them as long as they have dedication, punctuality and a good work ethic, the soft skills that are often overlooked when it comes to School-to-Career in the school systems.

According to Kiersz and Hoff (2020), of the 30 highest paying jobs in the future, eight of them are in the skilled trades. "The future can be built by those who know how to build – and by 'build', we mean install heating, venting, air conditioning; flooring; appliances; and all other modern amenities we rely on to keep our offices, homes and communities running. By 2028 there will be an estimated 3 million job vacancies in the skilled trades." (USA Today, 2021) According to the Home Improvement Research Institute, more than 60 percent of skilled trade professionals agree that there is a shortage of labor in the construction industry. The same study reports ongoing hiring challenges for professional contractors, with 40 percent of pros looking to expand their job site workforce. (PRNewswire, 2018). PRNewswire (2018) also states that "The U.S. Bureau of Labor Statistics (BLS) reports that the nation's need for workers in the skilled trades is increasing much faster than the growth of employment overall, according to a recent forecast. [An analysis] of BLS data projects [states that] we will experience a skilled trades gap of more than a half million jobs across construction-related fields by 2026."

This makes the future of School-to-Career not only preparing students for a college education, but returning school districts to stress the importance of preparing students for other careers as well. The August 2019 WorkIt! podcast titled *"Do I Need College"* directly addresses this issue. The answer is, on the surface, surprising. The answer is, "No." This is where there is a clarification made. Do students need to go to college to have a successful career? No. Do they need to be *educated*? Yes! There is a clear difference between college and education. To be educated means to be schooled in the information. You would need to take classes, participate in apprenticeships, keep up with new innovations and techniques within a trade, etc. None of these require a college degree. There are so many students that would flounder in a collegiate arena. These are the people who need to work with hands-on activities. These are the people who do not fit the mold of standardized testing and surveys. These are the people who need to be guided in the right direction because these people are the ones who are going to literally build our futures.

Appendix A

In this appendix, you will find activities that you can use in your classrooms to help embed School-to-Career within everyday activities. They are designated as E for elementary, M for middle school and H for high school.

1) **Adult Mentors** (M,H) – Students are assigned adult mentors from throughout the community. These mentors meet with the students on a regular basis (weekly) to have discussions with students. This is in a non-academic setting.

2) **Business Partnerships** (E,M,H) – Businesses throughout the community partner with the school system to help them with needs that the school(s) may have that they can contribute to. It creates a dialogue between schools and businesses to create a sense of community.

3) **Career Bingo** (E,M) – This is played like standard BINGO but, instead of B-I-N-G-O across the top, you would list five career clusters. Then in the boxes below, you would list an actual career that goes within the career cluster. For example: "B-12" would be replaced with "Health Science – Nurse". Please feel free to contact me at bonster67@hotmail.com if you would like me to send you a document with all of the cards and calling chips attached.

4) **Career Carnival** (E) – This activity would have carnival games with career tie-ins. There would be "Pin the tie on the Executive", Ring Toss with pegs representing jobs with higher paying jobs being worth more points, Career BINGO (see above), Career matching (see below), etc.

5) **Career Day** (M,H) – This would be a traditional Career Day where volunteers from the community (Business Partnerships) would come in and discuss their careers to either large or small groups within the school.

6) **Career Cluster of the Month** (E,M,H) – Feature a different cluster each month. Have this cluster displayed prominently. Do projects revolving around this cluster and encourage students to bring in articles, books, pictures etc., of people in this career cluster.

7) **Career Poetry Unit** (M,H) - This can be tied into a traditional ELA poetry unit. While students are learning about the various types of poetry, they create their poems about different careers or career clusters

8) **Career Portfolios** (M,H) – Students begin to create a portfolio of information and experiences that lead to careers that they are interested in. This would include a cover letter, resume', artifacts of involvement and experiences with potential career, etc.

9) **Celebrity Reader Day** (E) – This would be a day where members of the community (business partners) would come in and read about their career to elementary school students. This is also an opportunity for other local "celebrities" to participate including, the high school football team, high school band, etc. This is traditionally done in March to honor Dr. Seuss' birthday.

10) **Classified Ads Scavenger Hunt** (M) – Create a list of the career clusters and students have to search the classified ads for each. This could also be done by finding a certain number of classified ads from one specific career cluster. (See Appendix B)

11) **Cluster Collages** (E) – Students are assigned a specific career cluster and search through magazines for people in those career clusters, creating a collage. Students having difficulty finding specific career clusters can draw pictures instead.

12) **Commercials** (M,H) – Community members (business partners) create commercials about what their career is and what it entails, including "behind the scenes" where the general public does not necessarily go. These can be filmed by a high school media class and/or media club. They can then be organized into a menu with other careers for students to explore.

13) **Community Volunteerism** (E,M,H) – This is an opportunity for students to not only create connections within the community but, they can begin to learn a sense of philanthropy. It will make them feel as if they are invested in the community as well.

14) **Curriculum Applications to "Real Life"** (M,H) – Research shows that students will learn and retain more when they are able to make connections with the material. Connecting material to "real life" whenever possible will not only help them retain the information, but allow them to see the purpose and the "bigger picture" as to why they are learning the material.

15) **Externships** (M,H) – This is when a teacher goes out into the community and "job shadows" a career. The teacher then comes back and shares his/her experiences with the class. This is good for careers where a person job shadowing must be over 18 or a career where there would not be enough physical space to take an entire class.

16) **Field Trips** (E,M,H) – This is when you take a group of students to the site of a career and tour what the career entails and ask questions of the person who is participating in this particular career.

17) **Internships** (H) – Internships entail students going to an actual site on a regular basis to view, explore, and participate in actual activities that are associated with this career.

18) **Interest Inventories** (M,H) – Interest inventories can be good to start to narrow a focus down for students. There are many interest inventories available. The danger here is that

interest inventories can "pigeon hole" students and they are not to be set in stone. They are simply a starting point if a student is extremely confused and unsure of what his/her future is to be.

19) **Job Fair** (M,H) – This can be more traditional where employers will attend and meet with potential employees.

20) **Job Shadowing** (H) – Job shadowing is a short term activity. In contrast to an internship, job shadowing takes place for only one or two days. The participant follows someone around for the day watching and noting what is done for that career during typical working hours.

21) **Matching Game** (E,M) – This is played like "Concentration" is played. All cards are laid face down. The first player picks two cards. If the career and the cluster match, they keep the cards and go again. If not, they turn the cards back over and play continues to the left. The winner is the person with the most matches once all cards have been matched. Please feel free to contact me at bonster67@hotmail.com if you would like me to send you a document with all of the cards.

22) **Mock Interviews** (H) – Volunteers from the community (business partners) come to the school to "interview" students for a "job" that they are applying for. After the interview, the interviewer and the student discuss what the student has done correctly as well as areas for improvement. This can be done in person or virtually.

23) **Older Students Create Career Based Books for Younger Students** (M,H) – Through writing curriculum, students can create children's books about a variety of careers. These books can be bound and then shared with the elementary students for use in their classrooms, library and/or on "Celebrity Reader Day".

24) **Peer Mentors** (H) - This works the same way that "Adult Mentors" works with one exception. These mentors are high school students. They would meet with the students from the middle and elementary schools and serve in the same capacity as the Adult Mentors.

25) **Puzzles** (E,M,H) – Through the use of puzzle making programs (ex: puzzlemaker.com) you can create crosswords, word searches, etc. with vocabulary from the career clusters as well as careers themselves.

26) **Reflective Writing** (M,H) – Students can reflect and write about an experience that they had with a specific career or career cluster either within or out of the classroom.

27) **Research Project** (M,H) – This would be a traditional research project investigating a career. It can be made more challenging by requiring students to explore some of the lesser known careers within a cluster.

28) **Resume/Cover Letter Writing** (H) – Cover letter writing is an important skill that many people are not adept in doing. This can be part of a more traditional writing unit. Students also forget items to put in a resume. By starting early and reminding students to continually update their resume as they have experiences, it will create good habits for their futures.

29) **"Reverse" Career Day** (M,H) - Set it up similar to a "College Fair" where a variety of

careers are represented at "booths" and students who are interested in that career can ask that person questions and gain information regarding that specific career. There should be literature and hands-on activities available for participants.

30) **Speed Mentors** (H) – There would be tables set up and each person would be given a letter. The participants looking for mentors would be given a number. In five minute rounds, the potential mentee would go to each table speaking with the potential mentor, similar to "speed dating". When all of the rounds are over, the potential mentors list the top 3 people that they feel would be a good match and the mentees list the top 3 people that they feel would be a good match. People who match with each other would then have the opportunity to meet again for a longer amount of time to see if they would be a good mentor/mentee matchup. (See Appendix B)

31) **Students Teach a Lesson** (M) – Make the students responsible for teaching a lesson to the class based on a career/career cluster

32) **T-Chart** (H) – T-Chart is a good follow-up to the mock interview. The chart can be set up with "Effective" and "Ineffective" on either side of the T. As a way to debrief, students can list things that are considered "effective" ways to conduct yourself in an interview and things that are "ineffective" ways to conduct yourself in an interview. This can also be adapted to "pros" and "cons" of specific careers after investigating that career. (See Appendix B)

33) **Trade Books** (E,M,H) – Many books are available on many levels that focus on varieties of careers. These can be made available in the classroom and school libraries.

34) **Trucker Buddies** (E) – Students can become pen pals with a trucker. Trucker Buddy International can match your class up with a truck driver who will correspond with your students from the road. Their mission is "to put a face behind the steering wheel of trucks as they roll down the highway. Hoping that when children see a truck, they automatically think of their mentor who encourages them to excel in school and who helps create positive images of the trucking industry." Their website is https://truckerbuddy.org/.

35) **Videos** (E,M,H) – There are countless videos at a variety of levels available focusing on specific careers and career clusters.

36) **Vocabulary Chart** (E,M,H) – Similar to the Frayer Model chart, the student can utilize this chart with either a vocabulary term or an actual career (See Appendix B)

37) **Vocational Based Clubs** (M,H) – Teachers oversee school sponsored clubs that are career focused. These would include: Nursing Club, DECA, Future Farmers of America, etc.

38) **Wax Museum** (M,H) – Careers are investigated. There is a write-up created involving the career with information such as education, salary, etc. The students then dress up as a person in that specific career with the display. Other classes "tour" the "wax museum" viewing the exhibits.

39) **Who Am I?** (E) – The teacher or students create riddles with clues as to a specific career or career cluster. Students take turns guessing. This can also be done as a class "warm-up" or as a weekly contest.

40) **Writing Prompts** (M,H) – Embedding a writing prompt about a career, career cluster and/or career related experience is a great way to tie School-to-Career into the classroom setting.

Appendix B

Reproducible Sheets

Vocabulary Chart

Definition | # 3 Examples

Vocabulary Term

| 3 Examples | Illustration | 3 Questions |
| What it is Not | | & Answers |

T-Chart

Effective	Ineffective

Career Classifieds

Career Cluster	Attach Classified Ad

Speed Mentor Part 1 - Mentor Sheet

Number	Name	Notes

Speed Mentor Part 1 - Mentee Sheet

Letter	Name	Notes

Speed Mentor Part 2 - Mentor Sheet

My Top 3 Picks:

	Number	Name
1st		
2nd		
3rd		

Integrating Careers Into Your Classroom: Past, Present, Future

Speed Mentor Part 2 - Mentee Sheet

My Top 3 Picks:

	Letter	Name
1st		
2nd		
3rd		

References

50 states.com. (n.d.). *Connecticut – We're full of surprises.* Retrieved February 7, 2005 from http://www.50states.com/connecti.htm

Abt Associates, Inc. (2001). *Providing opportunities for all students: Findings from the process evaluation of Connecticut's school-to-career system.* Bethesda, MD: Abt Associates, Inc.

Abt Associates, Inc. (2003). *Process evaluation of Connecticut's school-to-career system: Year 2 final report.* Bethesda, MD: Abt Associates, Inc.

Abt Associates, Inc. (2003). *Summary of findings from the 2002-03 Connecticut school-to-career survey.* Bethesda, MD: Abt Associates, Inc.

Area Cooperative Educational Services. (n.d.). *School-to-work: Examples that work.* [Curriculum guide].

Area Cooperative Educational Services. (2004). School-to-Career notes.

Benson, A.N., & Blocher, D.H. (1975). The change process applied to career development programs. *Personnel and Guidance Journal, 53*(9), 656-661.

Bernard-Powers, J. (1917). *Vocational education act.* Retrieved September 14, 2004 from http://college.hmco.com/history/readerscomp/women/html/wh_038100_vocationaled.htm

Bishop, J. H. (1992). Why U.S. students need incentives to learn. *Educational Leadership, 49*(6), 17-18.

Bolman, L. G., & Deal, T. E. (1997). *Reframing organizations.* San Francisco: John Wiley & Sons, Inc.

CareerKey.org. (2021).

Brand, B., Partee, G., Kaufmann, B., & Wills, J. (2000). *Looking forward: School-to-work principles and strategies for sustainability.* Washington, DC: American Youth Policy Forum.

Bridges, W. (1991). *Managing transitions: Making the most of change.* Cambridge, MA: Perseus Books.

Castellano, M., Stringfield, S., & Stone, III, J.R. (2003). Secondary career and technical education and comprehensive school reform: Implications for research and practice. *Review of Educational Research, 73*(2), 231-272.

Charner, I., Macallum, K., & White, R. (1999, April). Measuring school-to-career effectiveness. *The High School Magazine,* p. 9-12.

Connecticut Business and Industry Association. (2000). *Employer's school-to-career pocket guide.* Hartford, CT: Connecticut Business and Industry Association.

Connecticut Business and Industry Association. (2003) *CBIA's education policies and practices.* Retrieved December 26, 2003 from http://www.cbia.com/ed/

Connecticut Business and Industry Association. (2004) *School-to-career: What is it?* Retrieved January 7, 2004 from http://www.cbia.com/ed/employers/whatisSTCforERS.htm

Connecticut Business and Industry Association. (2004). Sharpening Connecticut's competitive edge: Its workforce. *CBIA News 82(6)*, 1-6.

Connecticut Business and Industry Association. (2004) Website retrieved June 7, 2004 from http://www.intermediarynetwork.org/pdffiles/CBIASnapshot.pdf

Connecticut Business and Industry Association. (2004, July/August). *CBIA News.*

Connecticut Career Choices. (2004) *Pathways to innovation – about the program.* Retrieved June 7, 2004 from http://www.ctcareerchoices.org/detpages/about20.html

Connecticut Career Choices. (2204) *Pathways to innovation – about us.* Retrieved June 7, 2004 from http://www.ctcareerchoices.org/about.html

Connecticut Career Choices. (2004). Connecticut Career Choices Curriculum Development Meeting [Handout].

Connecticut Conference of Independent Colleges. (2005) *Office of Workforce Competitiveness (OWC) strategic plan for higher education and workforce development.* Retrieved June 5, 2005 from http://www.theccic.org/owc.shtml

Connecticut Department of Environmental Protection. (2005). *Connecticut's urban sites remedial action program.* Retrieved March 4, 2005 from http://dep.state.ct.us/pao/PERDfact/urban.htm

Connecticut Department of Labor. (n.d.) *At work for Connecticut's workforce.* Retrieved June 4, 2005 from http://www.ctdol.state.ct.us/rwdb/annual-rpt.pdf

Connecticut Department of Labor. (n.d.) *Connecticut Department of Labor workforce investment boards.* Retrieved June 5, 2005 from http://www.ctdol.state.ct.us/rwdb/rwdb.htm

Connecticut Department of Labor. (n.d.) *Connecticut school-to-career system FAQs.* Retrieved June 15, 2005 from http://www.ctdol.state.ct.us/schtocar/scctsys.htm

Connecticut Department of Labor. (n.d.) *Office for Workforce Competitiveness/CT's Workforce investment system.* Retrieved June 5, 2005 from http://www.ctdol.state.ct.us/rwdb/workforce.htm

Connecticut Department of Labor. (n.d.) *Workforce Investment Act (WIA).* Retrieved October 9, 2004 from http://www.infoline.org/InformationLibrary/docs/Workforce%20Investment%20Act20.htm

Connecticut Department of Labor. (n.d.) *Strategic Five-Year State Workforce Investment Plan.* Retrieved June 5, 2005 from http://www.ctdol.state.ct.us/rwdb/finalplan.pdf

Connecticut Learns. (1996). *Building Bridges from School to Career in Connecticut.* [Brochure].

Connecticut Learns. (1997). *Connecticut's plan for implementing a school-to-career system.* [Brochure].

Connecticut Learns. (1995). *A Report on the developments of the school-to-career system in Connecticut's schools.* [Brochure].

Connecticut Learns. (1998). *School-to-career system.* [PowerPoint].

The Connecticut Mentoring Partnership. (2004). *Connecticut's school-to-career program.* Retrieved December 20, 2004 from http://www.preventionworksct.org/cmp_schoolcareer.html

The Connecticut Mentoring Partnership. (2004). *The Corporate honor roll.* Retrieved December 20, 2004 from http://www.preventionworksct.org/cmp_forbiz.html

The Connecticut Mentoring Partnership. (2004). *Mentoring news and notes.* Retrieved December 20, 2004 from http://www.preventionworksct.org/cmp_home.html

Connecticut Regional Vocational-Technical School System. (2004). *Introduction.* Retrieved June 24, 2004 from http://www.cttech.org/central/about-us/intro.htm

Connecticut Regional Vocational-Technical School System. (2004). *Mission statement.* Retrieved June 24, 2004 from http://www.cttech.org/central/about-us/mission.htm

Connecticut Regional Vocational-Technical School System. (2002). *Where careers begin.* [Brochure].

Connecticut State Board of Education. (2004). *Connecticut technical high schools: Program of study* [Brochure].

Connecticut State Department of Education. (1998). *Building bridges from school-to-career in Connecticut.* [Brochure].

Connecticut State Department of Education. *Connecticut's Common Core of Learning.* Retrieved June 8, 2005 from http://www.state.ct.us/sde/dtl/curriculum/currkey2.htm

Connecticut State Department of Education. (2003). *Federal school-to-work quarterly report – Third quarter.*

Connecticut State Department of Education. (2004). *Career High School's strategic school profile.* Retrieved December 21, 2004 from http://www.csde.state.ct.us/public/der/ssp/sch0304/sr073.pdf

Connecticut State Department of Education. (2005). *Circular letter C-8.* Retrieved March 6, 2005 from http://www.state.ct.us/sde/circ/circ00-01/c-8.pdf

Connecticut State Department of Education. (2004). *New Haven's strategic school profile.* Retrieved December 20, 2004 from http://www.csde.state.ct.us/public/der/ssp/dist0304/dist060.pdf

Connecticut State Department of Education. (2004). *Plymouth's strategic school profile.* Retrieved November 19, 2004 from http://www.csde.state.ct.us/public/der/ssp/dist203/dist075.pdf

Connecticut State Department of Education. (2001). *School-to-career: A progress report.*

Connecticut State Department of Education. (2004). *Vocational-Technical School System's strategic school profile.* Retrieved December 21, 2004 from http://www.csde.state.ct.us/public/der/ssp/0304/vtdist001.pdf

Connecticut State Department of Education. (2005). *Terms and definitions.* Retrieved March 3, 2005 from http://www.csde.state.ct.us/public/der/ssp/terms.pdf

Connecticut State Department of Labor. *Job and career conneCTion.* Retrieved December 26, 2003 from http://www1.ctdol.state.ct.us/jcc/viewarticle.asp?intArticle=3&intPFV=1

Connecticut Technical Schools. (2004). *Program of studies (revised for the graduates of 2008).* [Brochure].

Coomer, C. (1999). Mastering context to deliver the Content. *High School,* 6(6), 19-21.

CT Mentor. *CT mentor.org.* (n.d.) Retrieved June 7, 2004 from

http://ctmentor.org/career/careercenter/whatis.asp

Danielson, C. (2002). *Enhancing student achievement: A framework for school improvement.* Alexandria, VA: Association for Supervision and Curriculum Development.

Decko, K.O. (2004). Working together for a competitive workforce. *CBIA News 82*(6), p. 2.

Doughty-Jenkins, B.M. (2003). *A history and evaluation of Plymouth, Connecticut's school-to-career program.* Unpublished doctoral field study, Central Connecticut State University.

Doughty-Jenkins, B.M. (2005). "Perspectives of School-to-Career Programs" *Techniques: Connecting Education and Careers,* (80(7), 36-39.

Duke, D. L. (2004). *The Challenges of educational change.* Boston: Pearson Education, Inc.

Eagle Forum. (n.d.). *Eagle forum.* [Brochure].

Eagle Forum. (1997). *Will your child be educated or trained in school-to-work?* [Brochure].

Edutopia, (2001) The School-to-Work Movement: Four Reports Look Back Retrieved February 5, 2021 from https://www.edutopia.org/four-reports-look-back-school-work-movement

Eligible Connecticut Rural Communities. (2005). Retrieved March 3, 2005 from

http://www.rurdev.usda.gov/ma/CTeligible.htm

Evans, Jr., J.H., & Burck, H. D. (1992). The effects of career education interventions on academic achievement: A meta-analysis. *Journal of Counseling & Development, 71*(6), 63-68.

Fouad, N. A. (1997). School-to-work transition: Voice from an implementer. *The Counseling Psychologist 25*(3), 403-412.

Fullan, M. (2001). *The NEW meaning of educational change.* New York: Teachers College, Columbia University.

Ginn, S.J. (1924). Vocational guidance in Boston public schools. *The Vocational Guidance Magazine, 3,* 2-9.

Gitterman, A., Levi, M., & Wayne, S. (1995). *Outcomes of school career development.* Ottawa: Canadian Guidance Counseling Foundation.

Glover, R.W., & Marshall, R. (1993). Improving school-to-work transition of American adolescents. *Teachers College Record, 94*(3), 588-610.

Goals 2000: Educate America Act of 1994, H.R. 1804, 103d Cong. (1994).

The Governor's Prevention Partnership website. Retrieved December 20, 2004 from http://www.preventionworksct.org/infostats/resstrategy.html

Gysbers, N.C., & Moore, E. J. (1975). Beyond career development: Life career development. *Personnel and Guidance Journal, 53*(9), 647-652.

Hamilton, M.A., & Hamilton, S.F. (1997). When is work a learning experience? *Phi Delta Kappan 79*(9), 682-689.

Harmon, H. (1999). Creating work-based learning opportunities for students in rural schools. *High School, 6*(6), 22-27.

Hansen, L. S., & Tennyson, W. W. (1975). A career management model for counselor involvement. *Personnel and Guidance Journal, 53*(9), 638-646.

High Schools.Com. (2005). *Connecticut high schools.* Retrieved March 4, 2005 from http://www.high-schools.com/connecticut/z.shtml

Hughes, K.L., Bailey, T.R., & Karp, M.M. (2002). School-to-work: Making a difference in education. *Phi Delta Kappan, 84*(4), 272-729.

Jiminez, L. (2020). Preparing American students for the workforce of the future. *Center for American Progress,* retrieved January 18, 2021 from https://www.americanprogress.org/issues/education-k-12/reports/2020/09/14/490338/preparing-american-students-workforce-future/

Johnson, L. S. (2000). The relevance of school to career: A study in student awareness. *Journal of Career Development, 26*(4), 263-276.

Kazis, R. (1999). Minding their business: What employers look for in school-to-career programs. *High School 6*(6), 15-18.

Kiersz, A. and Hoff, M. (2020). The 30 best high-paying jobs of the future. *Business Insider,* Retrieved from website January 17, 2021. https://www.businessinsider.com/best-jobs-future-growth-2019-3

Levine, D. (1994). The School-to-Work Opportunities Act of 1994: A flawed prescription for education reform. *Educational Foundations, 8*(3), 33-51.

Lynch, R. L. (2000). High school career and technical education for the first decade of the 21st century. *Journal of Vocational Education Research, 25*(2), 155-198.

Martin, J.R. (1992). *The Schoolhome: Rethinking schools for changing families.* Cambridge, MA: Harvard University Press.

McKinnon, B.E., & Jones, G.B. (1975). Field testing a comprehensive career guidance program, K-12. *Personnel and Guidance Journal, 53*(9), 663-667.

McLaren, J. (1994). *Life in Schools.* White Plains, N.Y.: Longmans.

Miller, J. V., & Benjamin, L. (1975). New career development strategies: Methods and resources. *Personnel and Guidance Journal, 53*(9), 694-699.

National Conference of State Legislatures. (2004). *Education program – School-to-work.* Retrieved May 15, 2004 from http://www.ncsl.org/programs/educ/Stw1.htm

National Vocational Educational (Smith-Hughes) Act, Public Law No. 347, Sixty-fourth Congress-S. 703 (1917).

New Haven Area Initiative for School-to-Work Opportunities. (1994). [Grant proposal].

New Haven Public Schools. (1998). *School to career opportunities; student, employer handbook.* [Brochure].

New Haven Public Schools. (n.d.). *Careers at a glance from the school to career clusters.* [Curriculum guide].

North Central Regional Educational Laboratory, School-to-Work Opportunities Act of 1994. Retrieved July 1, 2002 from

http://www.ncrel.org/sdrs/areas/issues/envrnmnt/stw/sw3swopp.htm

North Dakota Department of Career and Technical Education. (n.d.) Carl D. Perkins Career and Applied Technology Education Act of 1990. Retrieved September 15, 2004 from

http://www.state.nd.us/cte/services/prog-eval/perkins-act.html

Office for Workforce Competitiveness. (2004). *Connecticut career ladder advisory committee – Three year strategic plan.* [Handout].

Plymouth Board of Education. (2002). *Educational technology accomplishments 1998-present.*[Handout].

Plymouth Board of Education. (2002). *Plymouth school-to-career mission statement.* Plymouth Public Schools website http://plymouth.k12.ct.us

Poth, R. (2019). The future of work: How do we prepare our students? *Getting Smart.* Retrieved January 18, 2021 from

https://www.gettingsmart.com/2019/04/the-future-of-work-how-do-we-prepare-our-students/

PRNewswire, (2018). Lowe's commits to developing future skilled trade force with new employee pre-apprenticeship program. Retrieved January 16, 2021 from

https://corporate.lowes.com/newsroom/press-releases/lowes-commits-developing-future-skilled-trades-workforce-new-employee-pre-apprenticeship-program-02-22-18

Rowland, J.G. (Former Governor, State of Connecticut). (1999). Executive Order No. Fourteen-A.

Ryan, N. Carl D. Perkins Vocational and Technical Education Act. Retrieved September 15, 2004 from http://www.ihdi.uky.edu/kyada/carlperkins.htm

Sanders, J. R. (2000). *Evaluating school programs: An educator's guide.* Thousand Oaks: Corwin Press, Inc.

Schlafly, P. (1995). Is the government planning your child's career? *The Phyllis Schlafly Report 28*(3).

Schlafly, P. (1997). School-to-work and Goals 2000. *The Phyllis Schlafly Report 30*(9).

Schlafly, P. (1997). School-to-work will track train, not educate. *The Phyllis Schlafly Report 30*(8).

Schmoker, M. (2000). *Results: The key to continuous school improvement.* Alexandria: Association for Supervision and Curriculum Development.

School-to-Work Opportunities Act of 1994, PL 103-239, 108 Stat 568. (1994).

State of Connecticut, Act Concerning Education Aid *(Public Act No. 00-187),* (2000).

State of Connecticut, Act Concerning a Connecticut Strategic Workforce Plan (House Bill No. 5570), (2004).

State of Connecticut, Act Implementing the Connecticut Employment and Training Commission's Recommendations Concerning Connecticut's Information and Technology Workforce Development Needs (Public Act No. 01-193),(2002).

State of Connecticut, Act Updating Connecticut's Strategic Five-Year Workforce Investment Plan to Include an Education Component (Raised Bill No. 1344), (2001).

Thoni, R.J., & Olsson, P.M. (1975). A systematic career development program in a liberal arts college. *Personnel and Guidance Journal, 53*(9), 672-675.

Tiederman, D.V. (1975). Structuring personal integration into career education. *Personnel and Guidance Journal, 53*(9), 706-710.

Tozer, S., Violas, P., & Senese, G. (2002). *School and society: Historical and contemporary perspectives.* New York: McGraw-Hill.

Trucker Buddy https://truckerbuddy.org/

U.S. Department of Education. *Economic imperative for improving high schools.* Retrieved August 2, 2002 from http://www.ed.gov/offices/OVAE/HS/econimperissuebrief.html

U.S. Department of Education. (1996). *School-to-work yearbook.*

U. S. Department of Labor. *Workforce Innovation and Opportunity Act.* Retrieved February 5, 2021 from https://www.dol.gov/agencies/eta/wioa

U.S. Department of Labor. *The Workforce Innovation and Opportunity Act – Final Rules.* Retrieved February 5, 2021 from https://www.doleta.gov/WIOA/Docs/Top-Line-Fact-Sheet.pdf

U.S. Department of Labor. *WIOA Youth Program.* Retrieved February 5, 2021 from https://www.dol.gov/agencies/eta/youth/wioa-formula

U.S. Department of Labor Employment and Training Administration. (2000). *Evaluation of the school-to-work/out-of-school youth demonstration.*

U.S. Department of Labor Employment and Training Administration. (1994). *The School-to-work/youth apprenticeship demonstration: Preliminary findings.*

U.S. Department of Labor Employment and Training Administration. (1995). *Skills, standard and entry-level work.*

U.S. Department of Labor Employment and Training Administration. (n.d.) *School-to-work opportunities act: Out-of-school youth.* Retrieved February 12, 2004 from http://wdsc.doleta.gov/sga/sga/97-017sga.asp

USA Today. (2021). Do you have a future in the skilled trade (a sponsored story) Retrieved January 17, 2021 from https://www.usatoday.com/pages/interactives/sponsor-story/Future-in-skilled-trades/

United States Government Printing Office. (1918). *The Cardinal principles of secondary education.*

Wheatley, M.J. (1999). *Leadership and the new science.* San Francisco: Berrett-Koehler Publishers.

Wirth, A.G. *Charles A. Prosser and the Smith-Hughes Act.* (n.d.) Retrieved April 19, 2004 from http://www.cals.ncsu.edu/agexed/aee501/wirth.html

Wollman, M., Johnson, D.A., & Bottoms, J.E. (1975). Meeting career needs in two-year institutions. *Personnel and Guidance Journal 53*(9), 676-679.

Woodstock Academy website. Retrieved May 11, 2005 from http://www.woodstockacademy.org

Workforce Investment Act, Public Law 105-220, (1998).

WorkIt! August 2019 podcast "Do I Need College?" https://workitcareers.com/

Worthington, R.L., & Juntunen, C.L. (1997). The vocational development of non-college-bound youth: Counseling psychology and school-to-work transition movement. *The Counseling Psychologist, 25*(3), 323-363.

About Green Heart Living

Green Heart Living's mission is to make the world a more loving and peaceful place, one person at a time. Green Heart Living Press publishes inspirational books and stories of transformation, making the world a more loving and peaceful place, one book at a time.

Whether you have an idea for an inspirational book and want support through the writing process - or your book is already written and you are looking for a publishing path - Green Heart Living can help you get your book out into the world.

You can meet Green Heart authors on the Green Heart Living YouTube channel and the Green Heart Living Podcast.

www.greenheartliving.com

Green Heart Living Press Publications

Success in Any Season

*Growing Smarter: Collaboration Secrets
to Transform Your Income and Impact*

Transformation 2020

Transformation 2020 Companion Journal

The Great Pause: Blessings & Wisdom from COVID-19

The Great Pause Journal

Love Notes: Daily Wisdom for the Soul

*Green Your Heart, Green Your World: Avoid Burnout,
Save the World and Love Your Life*

www.ingramcontent.com/pod-product-compliance
Lightning Source LLC
Chambersburg PA
CBHW050351100426
42734CB00041B/3128